GREAT MYSTERIES

Mysteries of the Moon

OPPOSING VIEWPOINTS®

Look for these and other exciting *Great Mysteries: Opposing Viewpoints* books:

Alternative Healing
Amelia Earhart
Anastasia, Czarina or Fake?
Animal Communication
Artificial Intelligence
The Assassination of Abraham Lincoln
The Assassination of President Kennedy
Astrology
Atlantis
The Beginning of Language
The Bermuda Triangle
Bigfoot
Custer's Last Stand
The Devil
Dinosaurs
The Discovery of America
El Dorado, Land of Gold
The End of the World
ESP
Evolution
Jack the Ripper
King Arthur
Life After Death

Living in Space
The Loch Ness Monster
The Lost Colony of Roanoke
Miracles
Mysteries of the Moon
Noah's Ark
Pearl Harbor
Poltergeists
President Truman and the Atomic Bomb
Pyramids
Reincarnation
Relativity
Shamans
The Shroud of Turin
The Solar System
Stonehenge
The Trojan War
UFOs
Unicorns
Vampires
Voodoo
Water Monsters
Witches

GREAT MYSTERIES

Mysteries of the Moon

OPPOSING VIEWPOINTS®

by Patricia Haddock

Greenhaven Press, Inc.   P.O. Box 289009, San Diego, California 92198-9009

Library of Congress Cataloging-in-Publication Data

Haddock, Patricia.
    Mysteries of the moon : opposing viewpoints / by Patricia
    Haddock.
        p. cm. — (Great mysteries)
    Includes bibliographical references and index.
    Summary: Examines various viewpoints about the moon, its
origins, its powers, and its effect on people's day-to-day lives.
    ISBN 0-89908-094-4
    1.Moon—Juvenile literature.   [1. Moon.] I. Title.
II. Series: Great mysteries (Saint Paul, Minn.)
QB582.H33   1992
523.3—dc20   92-16423
                                   CIP
                                   AC

Contents

Introduction

This book is written for the curious—those who want to explore the mysteries that are everywhere. To be human is to be constantly surrounded by wonderment. How do birds fly? Are ghosts real? Can animals and people communicate? Was King Arthur a real person or a myth? Why did Amelia Earhart disappear? Did history really happen the way we think it did? Where did the world come from? Where is it going?

Great Mysteries: Opposing Viewpoints books are intended to offer the reader an opportunity to explore some of the many mysteries that both trouble and intrigue us. For the span of each book, we want the reader to feel that he or she is a scientist investigating the extinction of the dinosaurs, an archaeologist searching for clues to the origin of the great Egyptian pyramids, a psychic detective testing the existence of ESP.

One thing all mysteries have in common is that there is no ready answer. Often there are *many* answers but none on which even the majority of authorities agrees. *Great Mysteries: Opposing Viewpoints* books introduce the intriguing views of the experts, allowing the reader to participate in their explorations, their theories, and their disagreements as they try to explain the mysteries of our world.

But most readers won't want to stop here. These *Great Mysteries: Opposing Viewpoints* aim to stimulate the reader's curiosity. Although truth is often impossible to discover, the search is fascinating. It is up to the reader to examine the evidence, to decide whether the answer is there—or to explore further.

"Penetrating so many secrets, we cease to believe in the unknowable. But there it sits nevertheless, calmly licking its chops."

H.L. Mencken, American essayist

Prologue

Imagine a time when there was no electricity, no artificial source of light, no lanterns.

Imagine a time when the night's only light came from campfires and torches.

Imagine darkness all around. Hear the sounds of night creatures: Mice scurry, an owl hoots, mosquitoes buzz, crickets chirp . . . a wolf howls, and another answers.

You hear other sounds you cannot identify. Something slithers through the underbrush. A large animal paces softly just beyond the ring of light made by the campfire. You shiver even though the night is warm, and you wait for the moon to rise. Until that white orb of light edges over the horizon, you must remain at the campfire, where you are safe.

When the moon is round and full, you have all the light you need. You can hunt, fish, plant, and travel. All is well when the moon shines down on earth.

But when the moon vanishes for three nights each month, the world is dark and forbidding. No one ventures out. The only sanctuary is around the faint light of the campfire, and there you stay until the moon once again lights the night sky.

The moon has dominated the human imagination for tens of thousands of years. Over the ages, many ideas about the moon have come and gone. Some were farfetched. Some were correct. Some were just plain fanciful. This book explores many ideas about the moon—where those ideas came from, if they were right or wrong, and those that are still believed today.

(Opposite page) The moon's silent, nocturnal presence and dependable, regular cycle have inspired fear and wonder as well as a feeling of security and order from time immemorial.

One

What Did Ancient People Think of the Moon?

Early people did not understand the moon in the same way we do today. They did not have the scientific knowledge to fully comprehend what they observed in nature. They created myths to explain what or why something was happening. Many myths provided explanations for the mysteries of the moon—the bright, white ball in the sky that grew, shrank, disappeared, and reappeared with predictable regularity. Myths explained what the moon was, how it got into the sky, and what its purpose might be.

Moon Tales

Moon myths appear in just about every culture. Many of these myths try to explain the moon's phases—why the moon comes and goes and why it seems to change its shape from a thin crescent to a full circle.

An Australian aboriginal legend describes the moon as a fat old man named Bahloo. One night Bahloo coaxed two young women into letting him ride in their boat. When he tried to steal a kiss from one of the women, he fell into the water and for three full nights he was too ashamed to reappear. Finally Bahloo sneaked out as a little sliver of light,

(Opposite page) Ancient astronomer Claudius Ptolemy (center) contemplates the order of the cosmos. Day and Night are personified as male and female. Because time was measured by the moon's cycles Night holds a measuring scale and zodiac for marking times.

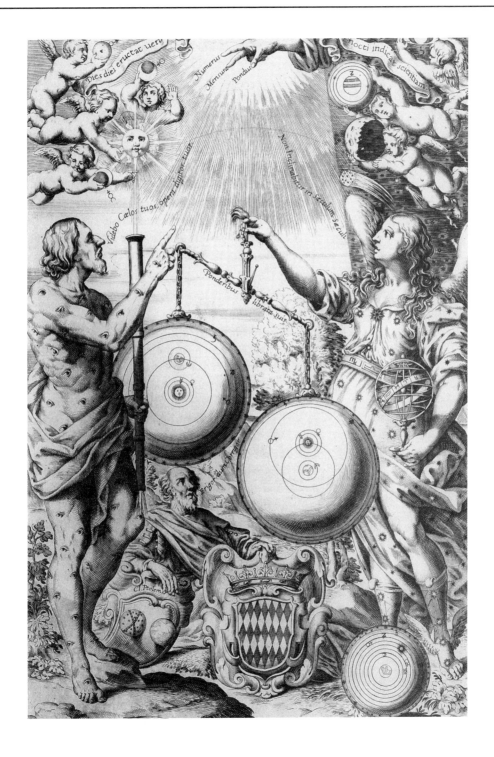

but it took another two weeks before he reappeared fully.

This myth describes the moon as a man. But another aboriginal legend says the moon is a woman who loves to go to parties. Each month, when she has partied too much and lost too much weight, she goes off to rest for three days.

Other myths do not portray the moon as either male or female. The Dakota people, native to North America, explain that the moon changes size and disappears because mice eat it, bite by bite, each night for two weeks. The moon then renews itself, growing bigger and bigger for two weeks, until the mice start to eat it again.

Today, people do not need tales of lusty old men and women or hungry mice to explain the moon's phases. We know that the shape of the moon does

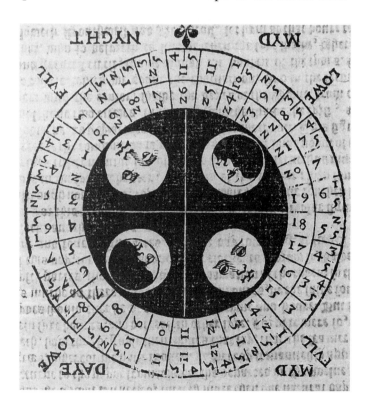

A table from a late Renaissance navigation chart shows how to keep track of time using the phases of the moon.

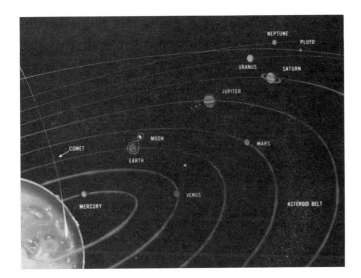

A map of the solar system shows how the moon revolves around the rotating earth while both revolve around the sun. The constantly changing positions of these three bodies create the apparent phases of the moon.

not really change. The moon only seems to change its shape because of the way the sun, earth, and moon move around each other.

The Moon's Phases

The sun is the center of our solar system. The earth moves around the sun and turns on its axis at the same time. This rotation of the earth creates day and night. As the earth turns, different parts of it face the sun. The sun also shines on the moon as it travels around the earth and strikes the moon at an angle that changes from night to night. Seen from earth, the moon appears to grow larger or smaller, depending on how much sun shines on it. We call the changing shapes of the moon its phases. Phases describe how much of the moon is lit by the sun and how much is in shadow.

The moon waxes as it grows from new to full and wanes as it shrinks from full to new. It is easy to tell if the moon is waxing or waning because the phases move from right to left. These are the moon's phases:

• New moon: The moon is completely in shadow and is invisible in the night sky.

• Waxing crescent: Only a thin sliver of moon on the right side is visible.

• First quarter: One half of the moon on the right side is lit by the sun.

• Waxing gibbous: The right three quarters of the moon is lit by the sun. (Gibbous comes from the Latin word for "humped" or "humpbacked.")

• Full moon: The entire face of the moon is lit.

• Waning gibbous: The left three quarters of the moon is lit.

• Last quarter: The half moon on the left is lit.

• Waning crescent: The sliver of moon to the left is visible.

Many societies call the phases of the moon by other names. Often the names reflect what is happening in the natural world during that phase. For instance, in the East Indies people call two phases of the moon "little pig moon" and "big pig moon." (The pig moons are the gibbous phases.) East Indians use these names because the tribe's pigs become excited by the amount of moonlight during these phases. The pigs often break out of their pens and escape into the fields. The phases are named after this regular event in tribal life.

In parts of Polynesia people use the expression "to twist" on the first night the waning moon appears because the crescent moon looks like a twisted thread. They say "the moon has cast a light" during the third and fourth nights after the new moon because these are the first nights a shadow can be seen in the moonlight. They call the thirteenth day after the new moon "egg" because the waxing gibbous moon looks like an egg.

Good Luck, Bad Luck

Many ancient people believed the moon's phases had the power to influence life on earth. That is why most cultures believed that for something to grow or flourish, it must be started or planted on the full moon.

"For the waxing moon's of good intent, but the waning moon brings sickness and death."

Plutarch, first-century Greek writer

"No direct link with the phases of the moon is visible."

Robert Eisler, *The Royal Art of Astrology*

Not everyone believed the full moon made plants grow. "Fig, apple, olive, and pear trees, as well as vines, should be planted in the dark of the moon, in the afternoon, when there is no south wind blowing," said the early Roman writer Cato.

Many people also believed that black magic and evil worked most strongly at the new moon. "For the waxing moon's of good intent, but the waning moon brings sickness and death," warned the first-century Greek philosopher Plutarch.

The Power of the Moon

Here are some beliefs about the power of the moon's phases, some of which are still held today:

• The Druids, who lived in ancient Ireland, Scotland, and Wales, believed the full moon brought prosperity. In Gaelic, the word for "full moon" is also the root word for "good fortune."

• A tribe in ancient Burma believed that a person who bathed in the light of a full moon would become strong.

• People in many cultures turned over the coins in their pockets or purses at the full moon to ensure abundance.

• Many people today believe that a wish made on the new moon will come true at the next full moon.

• In several cultures, marrying during the full moon is thought to bring the couple good fortune. many justices of the peace report an increase in the numbers of marriages at the time of the full moon.

• Not everyone thought the full moon brought prosperity or good luck. Many people from India believed that illnesses worsened at the full and new moons, and they thought the sick were more likely to die at these times.

• Some Native American tribes also believed the full moon was unlucky, and early Peruvian tribes often combined their symbol for the moon with their symbol for evil.

• Some cultures believed the full moon caused

Many cultures believed that the moon and its phases influenced life on earth. Many have considered the time of the full moon, for example, to be the best time for planting crops.

people to go mad or turned them into fierce animals or werewolves.

• The ancient Romans had their hair cut when the moon was waxing. They were afraid that if they cut it during a waning moon, they might go bald! Medieval people in Devonshire, England, on the other hand, believed that they should cut their hair during a waning moon. No fear of balding for these hardy English!

Today, many people who have read scientific research about the moon do not share these beliefs. They dismiss such ideas as superstitions.

Frightening Eclipses

Perhaps the most terrifying moon phenomenon for our ancestors was the eclipse. There are two types of eclipse: solar and lunar. Solar eclipses occur when the moon passes between the sun and the earth, hiding the sun from the view of a small area of the earth. During a total solar eclipse the sky gets dark even in the middle of the day. During a partial eclipse the sky looks like it does at dusk. Lunar eclipses occur when the moon moves into the earth's shadow (on the side of the earth away from the sun) and is blacked out; the moon seems to disappear from the sky. In every century, 237 partial and total solar eclipses and 154 lunar eclipses occur.

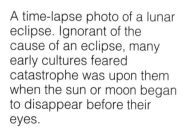

A time-lapse photo of a lunar eclipse. Ignorant of the cause of an eclipse, many early cultures feared catastrophe was upon them when the sun or moon began to disappear before their eyes.

Most ancient people were afraid of eclipses because they did not understand them and could not predict them. They did not realize that eclipses happen at regular intervals. Imagine how frightening it would be for those who know nothing of science if the sun started to vanish from the sky at midday, or if the moon were slowly extinguished at a time of the month when it should shine brightly.

Eclipses filled people's thoughts with questions: Where were the familiar lights in the sky going? Had people done something to make the gods so angry that they wanted to take away the sun and moon? Would the sun and moon come back or would the earth be plunged into darkness forever?

Hungry Monsters

Many cultures created myths to explain eclipses. In some cultures people believed that during an eclipse a monster was eating the sun or moon. In early China the monster was thought to be a dragon; in Southeast Asia it was a frog. A Paraguayan myth said that a lunar eclipse was caused by a jaguar attacking the moon, while a Native American legend said that it was caused by a giant, fierce dog that bit into the moon until it disappeared.

Many Native American tribes believed that during an eclipse, the moon was trapped by an evil spell. They offered prayers and gifts to the gods to free the moon. People everywhere lit torches to ensure that light of some kind would continue on earth in case the sun or moon never returned.

The Chinese and Southeast Asians grabbed their drums and brass kettles and raised a terrible noise to frighten away the "demon" who was destroying the moon. Early Peruvian warriors shot arrows into the sky to help the eclipsed sun or moon fend off the ravenous creature trying to eat it. More recently, modern warriors in Cambodia have fired rifles in the air to scare off the monster.

Some early peoples viewed eclipses as omens—

"There is a definite connection between the moon and the water in the earth. . . . Root crops . . . sown in the waxing phase of the moon can more strongly take up into themselves the watery element than those sown in the waning phase of the moon."

Madam L. Kolisko, *The Moon and Growth of Plants*

"When we believe a correlation exists between two things, we are more likely to notice and recall confirming than disconfirming instances."

D.G. Meyers, *Social Psychology*

warnings of things to come. Twenty-five hundred years ago an eclipse ended a war mid-battle because the combatants feared it would bring a disaster even worse that the battle they were fighting. The Medes and Lydian peoples of Asia Minor were engaged in a bloody melee—just one of many that had occurred during their six-year war. According to fifth-century B.C. Greek historian Herodotus, "Just as the battle was growing warm, day was suddenly changed into night." Both sides viewed the eclipse as an omen that the war should be ended, and they agreed to a truce.

As more sophisticated methods for marking the passage of time developed, a few people realized that monsters and omens had nothing to do with eclipses. Because the people discovered the movement patterns of the sun, moon, and earth, they realized that eclipses occurred regularly and could be predicted.

Predicting Eclipses

The early Roman emperor Claudius understood what eclipses were and how to predict them. When an eclipse was due on his birthday, he worried that superstitious Romans would think he was ill-omened. Taking the initiative, Claudius announced that an eclipse was about to happen and explained what it was. He had a successful birthday party, and no one thought badly of him when the sun was eclipsed during the festivities.

The explorer Christopher Columbus also used his knowledge of eclipses to his advantage. In 1503 his ship ran aground in the area now called the Caribbean. At first the native people gave his crew all the food they wanted, but they soon stopped doing so because Columbus' men were so rowdy.

Columbus knew he had to feed his crew to avoid a mutiny. He also knew that an eclipse was due, so he asked the natives for food and threatened to make the moon's light go out if they did not com-

The first-century Roman emperor Claudius learned how to predict eclipses and use them to his advantage.

ply. The people thought he was bluffing and refused to provide more food. Then, right on schedule, a lunar eclipse occurred. The natives believed Columbus had made the moon go dark, and they gave him the food he wanted.

Throughout history, there were people such as Claudius and Columbus who understood what the moon was and how and why it moved the way it did. But there were many more people who had fantastical and mythological ideas about the moon and its movements. Some people even believed that the moon was a powerful deity—a god or goddess—that was worthy of worship and sacrifice.

Christopher Columbus predicts a lunar eclipse as the natives of a Caribbean island listen in terror. The natives thought Columbus caused the eclipse, and, fearful of him, gave him and his crew the supplies the explorers had demanded.

Two

What Powers Did People Believe the Moon Had?

Early people believed the moon, sun, and stars were deities who controlled human destiny. They thought the moon influenced the growth of population and food, the two most important factors in their survival. Therefore, they worshiped the moon in the hope that it would bring them good fortune. Some cultures thought the moon deity was male, others that it was female.

Lunar Symbols

Symbols for the moon appear in a wide range of cultures. Scientists have found the earliest symbol for the moon deity engraved on stone pillars at many ancient sites. They believe the symbols were carved at the end of the Stone Age, around 8000 B.C. Cave dwellers also etched moon symbols on the walls of their caves and on reindeer bone, ivory, and stones they used as lunar calendars.

Some early people worshiped special stones because they thought the stones represented the moon god or goddess's holy presence on earth. These stones were often black or white, to symbolize the light or dark phases of the moon. Cones of sandstone dedicated to the moon have been found at Mount Sinai in the Middle East. The moon goddess

(Opposite page) NASA scientist John Brandt examines some ancient American Indian stone carvings depicting the moon and a distant star. The moon has held a prominent place in almost every culture throughout history.

The moon was the ancient Assyrians' chief deity. They have left many depictions of a moon tree, representing the fertile full moon, flanked by a winged lion, representing the sun, and a unicorn, representing the moon. In this carving, the king is about to slay the lion, a sun-symbol, perhaps to show that the moon, not the sun, is lord of the heavens.

was probably worshiped there long before Moses was believed to have received the Ten Commandments. Melanesians, in the southwestern Pacific, worshiped circular and crescent-shaped stones, which stood for the full and crescent moons.

Some early societies associated certain trees with the moon. A sacred moon tree appears in many ancient religious artifacts. The moon tree is often laden with fruit or lights, like a Christmas tree, or ribbons, like a Maypole. For centuries in northwest India, people have plucked ripened moon-tree fruit by moonlight to make a drink they believe will give them wisdom and immortality. Artifacts from Assyria contain etchings of the moon trees standing between a winged lion and a unicorn. One animal is walking toward the tree and represents the waxing moon; the other is walking away from the tree and represents the waning moon. The tree itself symbolizes the full moon, which brings forth new life.

Horns are another kind of ancient lunar symbol. One horn represented the new moon, two horns the full moon. Moon goddesses and gods in many cultures are depicted with horns or are accompanied by a full or crescent moon. Rulers from early cultures—the Celts, Vikings, and Egyptians, for instance—often wore horned headdresses that symbolized the crescent moon. Sometimes the rulers themselves were assumed to be gods.

The snake has long been a lunar symbol. The snake moves secretively into and out of holes in the earth, vanishing and reappearing, as does the moon in the sky. Like the moon, the snake symbolizes the power of renewal because it sheds its skin for a new one. The snake is cold-blooded and sometimes deadly, characteristics often associated with the dark phase of the moon. Many cultures depicted the serpent as part of the dark manifestations of the moon deity.

The Moon Man

A common myth in primitive societies was that the young moon man first appeared as a bright sliver of light in the night sky to fight the devil who had eaten his father, the old moon. As the waxing moon man became stronger and bigger, he was better able to defeat the devil (usually symbolized as a dragon). When he became a full moon, the moon man came down to earth to reign as a good and powerful king. He taught his people when to plant and harvest crops, and he dispensed wisdom and justice. After a few days, the devil would regain his strength and chase the moon man into the sky again. He bit more and more of the waning moon man each night until the moon was eaten up, and the sky would become dark for three nights. Then another young moon man would appear as a sliver of light in the night sky to take up the twenty-nine-day chase with the devil once more.

In Babylonia around 1800 B.C., the moon god Sin was known as the god of wisdom. His familiar name was Illuminator. The Babylonians believed his light illuminated the traps set by evil spirits so that men and women could avoid falling into them.

Another Babylonian myth described the moon god as an old man with dark blue skin. At night he sailed through the sky in a boat. This moon god did multiple duty, since he was also the god of time, the dispenser of dreams and prophecies, and the god of evil and darkness.

The Moon God Thoth

In ancient Egypt lunar worship was one of the earliest religions. Thoth was a moon god and the god of science, literature, wisdom, and inventions. He is often shown as an ibis (a water bird) with a crescent. Every night, the story goes, Thoth climbs into his boat and sails across the sky. As the month goes by, monsters slowly eat him. Valiant defenders attack the monsters and make them disgorge Thoth so that he may reappear as a waxing moon at the beginning of each month.

Iranians who lived in the sixth century B.C. called the lunar deity the Great Man. They believed he was a person who lived on the moon exactly as they did on earth. When an Iranian king declared himself the moon man, reincarnated on earth as the king of Iran, he created a dynasty and declared that all kings descended from that dynasty would be the reincarnated moon man. Some of these kings wore horns that represented the crescent moon.

By the thirteenth century, people who thought the moon was a male god no longer believed that he was actually walking on earth as a man. However, some rulers believed they still had a divine connection with the moon god. For example, Mongolian emperor Genghis Khan claimed he was the moon's representative on earth. He told the people in his kingdom that one of his ancestors was a king whose

An ancient Babylonian drawing of the moon god Sin sailing the heavens in his crescent-moon-shaped boat.

wife was impregnated by a moon ray.

Other kings have claimed such a divine origin: The leader of the Einu in Polynesia was called the Lord of the Moon, and even today the people say "The moon has fallen" when the chief of Samoa dies.

The Moon Goddess

Although many people throughout history have worshiped a lunar god, some believed the moon was female. Many historians believe the worship of a moon goddess did not really become common until some ancient religions began to promote sun-god worship.

Before sun worship, the earliest primitives thought the moon was the most powerful deity. Because in many cultures males were thought to be more important than females, the people naturally assumed that the most powerful deity, the moon, was male. When people began to worship the sun god, religious leaders reasoned that the two male gods would be threats to each other and would be in constant conflict. But if the moon were a goddess, she could rule over moon attributes such as water and fertility without being a threat to the sun god. It was believed that she would not try to fight someone stronger than she.

Ishtar of Babylonia was one of the earliest moon goddesses. Her name was used as far back as 1478 B.C., but historians know that the Semitic (early Middle Eastern) people had been worshiping her for hundreds of years before then. The Babylonians believed Ishtar was the daughter of the lunar god Sin. As Sin became old and weak, his daughter became stronger—until she became the lunar goddess. This myth helped religious leaders explain to their followers how a lunar god could turn into a lunar goddess.

A North American Indian myth tells the story of an old lady and her beautiful granddaughter who

The ibis-headed Egyptian moon god Thoth also ruled wisdom, science, and communication.

lived alone on the moon. When the granddaughter
asked why they were alone, the grandmother said
that only she had the power to protect herself and
her granddaughter from the evil spirit that had destroyed everyone else. The granddaughter thought
that surely others had survived, so she decided to go
in search of them. She left her home and traveled
through the heavens.

On the tenth day of her search she came across
a cabin in which eleven brothers, all hunters, were
living. The youngest one married her, but he died
soon after she gave birth to a son. She then married
the next youngest, who also died. She continued to
marry each of the surviving brothers in turn, until
the eldest was the only brother still alive. They married, but she soon tired of him.

She sneaked out the west window of the cabin
one day, taking her dog and disappearing into the
earth. She reappeared in the east, where she met an
old fisherman—the person who had made the earth.
He told her to go west, and off she went.

Her husband went searching for her, first into
the western sky, then into the eastern sky. At last, he
also came upon the fisherman.

"Your wife went to the west," said the fisherman. "You will pursue her forever, but you will
never catch her. The nations that will one day be
upon this earth will call you Gizhigooke, he who
makes the day."

Explaining Natural Phenomena

This story of the husband's pursuit of his wife
from the eastern sky to the western sky tells how
the sun was born and explains why the sun never
catches the moon. The people who believed this
myth counted eleven moons in a year—one for each
of the eleven brothers.

One of the earliest creation stories about Mother
Moon and Mother Earth was told in cultures as di-
verse as those in Scandinavia, China, India, and

Greece. The myth says that the earth and the moon were created from the "world egg." When it cracked open, the moon popped out and split in half. One-half stayed in the sky as the moon; the other half became the earth. The world egg—the mother egg—was where all life came from.

Belief in the femininity of the moon has existed at one time or another in just about every culture and religion throughout the world. Early people considered women to be of the same nature as the moon: Not only did women swell up with pregnancy much as the moon appears to swell up each month, but women's monthly menstrual cycles are approximately the same length of time as the moon's monthly cycle. For primitive people, these two facts were enough to prove the connection between women and the moon.

The Moon Goddess and Fertility

The moon, women, and the mother goddess were also connected through fertility. Primitive cultures from South America, Africa, Asia, and Europe believed the moon had a fertilizing power. Many primitive people believed that life could not propagate or grow without the help of the moon, that a seed was like a stone without power of its own. The power to continue the species had to be bestowed by the god or goddess of fertility. This deity could turn seeds into plants that would produce fruits and vegetables. In cultures where people believed that only the moon goddess had the power to make seeds grow, the people held ceremonies and holidays in her honor and prayed to her for healthy crops.

This power was not limited to the plant kingdom. It also influenced animals and people. In ancient Rome, for example, one of the goddess Diana's temples was located at Lake Nemi. At the full moon in August, women walked in procession to her temple at the lake and left gifts to ensure their

Like many other moon goddesses, the Roman Diana was also a fertility goddess. In this painting from the Renaissance, she wears the characteristic crescent-moon crown.

fertility. In ancient Nigeria people believed the Great Moon Mother sent the Moon Bird to bring babies to women who wanted them.

"The Universal Goddess as Birth Giver is among the oldest of the great divinities known to the myths of the world," writes author Barbara G. Walker. The goddess is "represented everywhere in shrines dedicated to local mother goddesses."

Women of many cultures called upon the moon to help them through their birthing labor. One of the midwife's main duties was to call down the assistance of the moon. Walker writes, "The moon is so closely linked to birth that in many societies it was called the great midwife."

The moon as a fertility goddess was known by

many names. Among the goddesses connected to fertility and the moon were Cybele in Phrygia, Artemis in Greece, Isis in Egypt, Diana in Rome, and Astarte in Phoenicia.

The Moon Goddess and Water

Primitive tribes, such as the Celts from early Europe and Great Britain, believed the moon goddess controlled the ebb and flow of water. She controlled the dew, the rain, tides, rivers, and springs. Members of farming and fishing tribes performed many rituals to persuade the goddess to bring rain for their crops and to calm the seas in time for their fishing expeditions. The rainmakers who chanted and danced to the moon goddess were usually women, since people thought women had a natural understanding of the cyclical rhythm of the moon and could better communicate to the lunar deity.

In Greece the moon goddess was called All-Dewy-One, and people had a dew ceremony every year in her honor. Dew was a symbol of fertility, and agricultural societies knew that damp earth created new vegetation.

In the Yucatan and Campeche regions of Mexico and in Guatemala, the moon goddess was called Ix Chel. She controlled water and also possessed the knowledge of healing. The Central American people believed that Ix Chel occasionally flooded the earth with walls of water to cleanse it and create new life.

Sometimes called the eagle woman, Ix Chel is often shown wearing a crown of feathers. She would fly to the feet of those who were ill, bringing them a drink made with finely ground powder of crab, turkey broth, guava tips, papaya, the sap of a rubber tree, and honey mead. She gave this magic drink to sick people to make them well.

The traditional sun-moon myth of the Eskimos of North America is that soon after the earth was formed, the king of the earth became so powerful

In ancient Egypt, Isis personified the moon, motherhood, and fertility. This statue shows her wearing the crescent-and-full-moon crown and nursing her son, the divine child Horus.

that he could fly up to the heavens whenever he wished. One time he took his beautiful sister along, as well as fire to create the sun. After a while the king began to treat his sister cruelly. In a fit of anger one day, he burned the side of her face. She escaped from the sun and became the moon, and her brother chases her across the sky. As the burned side of the face turns toward the earth, the moon grows dark; as her other side faces earth, the moon's light shines.

The Mayans believed the moon was a source of knowledge and an example of female independence. In their myth, the moon and the sun were equally bright when they were first born. The sun god became attracted to the moon goddess and wanted to win her love. But her grandfather was strict and guarded her closely. To trick him, the sun borrowed the body of a hummingbird and flew to his beloved moon goddess. As she was giving him a drink made from flower nectar, the sun suddenly was shot with pellets that pierced his wings. The goddess helped him into the sky as they tried to escape the anger of her grandfather.

But the grandfather sent a bolt of lightning into the heavens, killing the goddess. Thousands of

Not only ancient people believed the moon to be feminine. These two photos of the full moon taken through a telescope in 1894 show the viewer how to discern the figure of the lady in the moon.

dragonflies hovered around her body for days, making such a bright light that even the sun was blinded. And when the dragonflies left her side, the moon was alive again!

The sun god and moon goddess married, but the sun soon became jealous. He thought his younger brother was spending too much time with the moon goddess. He accused her of being unfaithful and threw her out of the sky. Angry and hurt, she landed in the grass on earth. A vulture flew by and took her to the king of the vultures atop the highest mountain. The sun felt sorrow for his behavior, and he missed his wife. He set out to find her, and when he did, he begged her to return home with him. She did, but he soon became jealous again. "If I cannot have you, no one else will," he shouted. He hit her, causing her beautiful face to be scarred and her light to grow dim.

The moon goddess was so angry that she leaped away into another part of the heavens. She never again shone as brightly as the sun, but she did have her own route through the sky and could move around as she wanted without the sun's bothering her.

Gifts of Knowledge

This myth, the Mayans believed, showed one of the many gifts of knowledge the moon goddess gives to women: They must be free to come and go as they please—and even to disappear sometimes, just as the moon does every month.

The ancient Hebrew tribes venerated the moon and believed in its power. Alga, meaning "moonlight," was one of the Hebrews' secret names for their god.

Certain Hebrew prophets spent much of their time denouncing lunar worship and the wearing of lunar amulets. But in trying to eradicate moon worship, they faced a difficult task. A passage from the Book of Jeremiah, one of the Hebrew holy books, demonstrates the strong hold lunar worship had on the ancient Hebrews, especially women:

> All the men who knew that their wives offered incense to alien gods, and all the women who were standing there . . . answered Jeremiah as follows: "We have no intention of listening to this word you have spoken to us in Yahweh's name, but intend to go on doing all we have vowed to do: offering incense to the Queen of Heaven [the moon goddess] and pouring libations in her honour, as we used to do, we and our fathers, our kings and our leaders, in the town of Judah and in the streets of Jerusalem: We had food in plenty then, we lived well, we suffered no disasters. But since we gave up offering incense to the Queen of Heaven and pouring libations in her honour, we have been destitute and have perished either by sword or by famine." (Jeremiah 44:25-29)

Sun Goddess, Moon God

Most early cultures worshiped a sun god and a moon goddess. But the Toba people of Argentina have for centuries worshiped a sun goddess and a moon god. They still believe that all Toba women once lived in the heavens. The women made long ropes to climb down to earth in search of food. There they saw men, who were covered with fur and walking on their hands and knees. When the men saw the ropes hanging from the sky, they leaped into the air and bit them in half. The women could no longer reach the ropes to return to their home in the sky, and they had to remain on earth with the men.

One woman named Akewa had remained in the sky, and she became the sun goddess. In winter she is a young woman, and she begins her daily walk in the eastern horizon. She climbs high across the sky, her rays lighting the earth. As the months go by, she becomes older and slower. It takes her more time to move across the sky, and that is why summer days are longer than winter days.

Each day, when Akewa vanishes, the moon god appears in the night sky. He is an old man with a glowing pot belly that he got from eating too much. His stomach is so big that it is hard for him to sleep. At the beginning of the month, he lies on his right side, and that is when people on earth can see his crescent light in the sky. As the days go by the moon man keeps turning slowly, so that more of his glowing stomach can be seen. When he is lying flat on his back, the people see a full moon.

Then a jaguar leaps into the sky and begins to take bites of the moon man's stomach—one bite every night—until the moon man disappears for three nights. After three nights, he regains his strength by eating a lot, and people can see the thin light of this stomach again.

The Bushmen of Africa also believe in a sun goddess and a moon god. They believe that when the sun goddess becomes angry with the moon god, she pierces him with her rays until most of his face disappears. He begs her to save a tiny piece of him for his children. From that sliver of light, which is so thin people cannot see it on earth, a new moon grows.

Jack and Jill

Even the nursery rhyme about Jack and Jill originated with moon mythology! The Scandinavians believed in the sun goddess (Sol) and her brother, the moon god (Mani). In the Norse tale, Bil (pronounced something like Jill in Old Norse) and Hijuki (pronounced similarly to Jack) were walking to a well with a pole and a bucket to get water. Mani causes Hijuki and Bil to fall down the hill. In Old Norse, the name Hijuki comes from jakka (to pile together), and Bil comes from *bilau* (to break up or dissolve). Mythologists say that when Jack (Hijuki) and Jill (Bil) fall down the hill, they symbolize the waxing and waning of the moon. And the

"The moon has often been thought of as the divine eye of god through which the heavenly host can see and know all, making the moon a kind of divine judge and jury rolled into one."

Paul Katzeff, *Full Moons*

"Today the sun gods reign, and they caution us about moonlight. French peasants consider it dangerous to sleep in moonlight. Mussolini feared contamination by moonlight. The Bedouins are warned not to gaze fixedly upon the moon."

Peter Steinhart, *Audubon*, September 1989

The millennia-old moon myths seem to be buried deep in the psyche of modern people, too. This drawing depicts a modern woman's dream in which the phases of the moon are personified as mermaids standing before an enthroned Egyptian-like, animal-headed god. The moon's connection with ocean tides may be symbolized in the mermaids, who may represent the moon's phases. As the moon waxes, the scaly covering of the mermaid falls away; as it wanes, the scales cover her again.

water image—filling the bucket and then spilling it—symbolizes the belief that the moon's phases influenced rainfall.

Whether people believed in a moon god or a moon goddess, they believed that this deity had two personalities. The light or white side of the moon represented its wisdom and control over fertility, growth, and abundance. Its dark side symbolized a bloodthirsty personality that could cause horrible destruction.

The Dark Side of the Moon

Writer M. Esther Harding has studied ancient rituals and beliefs concerning the moon. She explains how the ancients viewed the moon goddess's personality: She "lived her life in phases. . . . In the upper world phase, corresponding to the bright moon, she is good, beneficent. In her other phase, corresponding to the time when the moon is dark, she is cruel, destructive, and evil."

Statues and etchings painted black or white symbolized the two personalities of the moon goddess. The statue of an ancient Mexican moon goddess, for example, shows a woman whose face is painted half black, half white. It represents the light and dark (good and evil) phases of the moon. Similarly, the upper half of the face of the Greek goddess Erinyes is painted white; the part of the face from the mouth down is painted black. The aboriginal Ainu people of Japan still portray the moon goddess dressed in black and white clothing, and Isis of Egypt has two manifestations. In one she is white to symbolize the moon's waxing phase; in the other she is black for the waning phase.

Two Separate Beings?

While some societies believed in a moon deity with a split personality, most early cultures saw the moon as two separate beings. The Greeks, for example, called the goddess of the light aspects of the moon Aphrodite. The dark aspects of the moon were represented by Hecate, the patroness of sorcery and queen of hell. She could control people's thoughts, so wizards and fortune-tellers worshiped her. The early Greeks believed that whenever Jason, Aphrodite's son, wanted the help of magic powers, he would call upon Hecate, who had power over the unconscious. Dark moon goddesses in other cultures included Anat, the moon goddess of the Phoenicians, who often killed for pleasure; and Kali Ma, the Hindu goddess who wore dead bodies for clothing and skulls for jewelry.

Black or white, good or evil, the moon has been an important part of people's lives for thousands of years. Gods and goddesses have been honored and feared, loved and hated—and even given human personalities, names, and histories so that people could better relate to them.

"The moon has often been thought of as the divine eye of god through which the heavenly host can see and know all," wrote author Paul Katzeff, "making the moon a kind of divine judge and jury rolled into one."

Three

Where Did the Moon Come From?

For thousands of years people have been fascinated and mystified about how the sun, stars, earth, and moon originated. Until the invention of instruments that have helped scientists understand more about the cosmos, people could only guess how the universe was formed and what it was made of. Those guesses became myths, which people believed. Different cultures believed different myths. People were especially curious about the relationship between the earth and the moon.

Myths and Theories About the Earth

Since the earth is our home, it is only natural that people have wondered about where it comes from and how it moves through space. Thales, a Greek philosopher who lived more than two thousand years ago, believed the earth floated on water. Anaximander, another Greek who lived at that time, believed the earth was in a cylinder, floating in space. He said the earth sat at one end of the cylinder, the sky at the other.

The Chinese and Hebrews thought the earth stood on pillars, while the people of India said the earth sat on the back of a giant elephant that was carried through space on the back of a turtle. The

turtle, they believed, swam around in an endless sea.

For many centuries, among educated people, the most popular theory about the universe was based on scientific observation, not myth. These people believed the earth stood still and the sun, moon, and stars moved around it. This theory was comforting. People felt they were standing on something solid that was the center of the universe. Today, however, we know that theory is not true.

Science Intervenes

In the early sixteenth century a great scientist named Nicolaus Copernicus promoted the theory we believe today about how the planets, moon, and sun moved. He said the sun, not the earth, is the center of the universe. The planets, moon, and stars travel around it. This theory is called a heliocentric, or sun-centered, theory.

Copernicus was not the first person to come to this conclusion. About twenty-three hundred years ago, the Greek astronomer Aristarchus said the same thing. But Aristarchus's ideas were largely ignored in favor of the earth-centered concept. It was Copernicus's writings that eventually persuaded scientists and that have guided the world's view of the universe even up to today.

Modern scientific inventions, such as telescopes and space capsules, have enabled scientists to get a closer look at the moon. Close observation has enabled them to come up with scientific theories that may answer the many questions people have wondered about for ages. Even with all of today's scientific knowledge, however, many questions remain to be answered.

The Birth of the Heavenly Bodies

Where did the moon come from? How does it stay up in the sky without falling down? What is it made of? Just about every culture has created myths

In the early sixteenth century, astronomer Nicolaus Copernicus started the so-called Copernican revolution by theorizing that the earth revolved around the sun.

and theories to answer these questions.

A legend in central India tells the story of Kawachi and Kuhrami, the first boy and girl on earth. One day Kawachi and Kuhrami went fishing and caught a big fish.

"Let us out!" voices called from inside the fish.

Kawachi and Kuhrami cut the fish open and found the sun and the moon inside. They took the sun and the moon home to live with them.

The sun and the moon soon married and had many children they called stars. After many years, so many stars were in the house that there was no room for Kawachi and Kuhrami.

"There is no room for all of us anymore," said Kawachi.

"Yes," said Kuhrami. "We have enjoyed your company for many years, but now you and your children, the stars, must leave." So the sun, the moon, and the stars moved up to the sky where they had plenty of room.

A Nigerian myth relates that the sun and moon were husband and wife who lived in a kraal, a group of huts surrounded by a fence.

One day the sun came to the ocean. "Come visit me," the sun said, "and bring the creatures that live with you."

The ocean readily accepted the sun's invitation and flooded into the kraal. But it did not stop coming. Tons of water and all the fishes in the sea flooded into the kraal. The sun and the moon had to leap into the sky to avoid being drowned. They decided to leave the earth to the ocean, and they remained in the sky where they were safe.

Anansi

Another myth, from West Africa and Haiti, tells of Anansi and his six sons. Anansi loved his sons very much and wanted to give a gift to each of them. One day he went into the forest, where he came upon a bright light of pure white, illuminating the gloom of the woods. Anansi carried the light home to give to one of his sons. But which son?

When each of Anansi's sons saw the light, he wanted it for his own. The sons began fighting to see who would have the wonderful gift. Nyame, the sky god, heard their quarrels and snatched up the light.

"None of you has ever fought before," Nyame said. "But since the light came among you, you have done nothing but fight." With that, Nyame threw the light into the sky with a tremendous force, and there it stayed to light the night sky.

These imaginative stories about the origin of the moon served an important purpose to people living hundreds of years ago. The people wanted to understand how the bright objects in the sky got there, what they were made of, and how they managed to keep from falling to the earth. Myths provided those answers.

Theories About the Moon's Origin

In the midtwentieth century the development of rocket power led to actual physical exploration of the moon. For the first time there really was a man on the moon—in fact, there were two: In 1969 astronauts Neil A. Armstrong and Edwin E. Aldrin Jr., became the first men to walk on the moon. The astronauts picked up moon rocks to bring back to earth so scientists could study them.

Scientists have learned a lot from carefully testing the samples. These studies have helped scientists determine that many lunar myths and assumptions, even those held by scientists as recently as thirty years ago, are wrong.

Yet even today, after two decades of study and with vast scientific knowledge and tools, many unanswered questions remain. One of the most important ones is: Where did the moon come from and how did it get into the night sky?

Modern scientists began seriously studying the

U.S. astronaut Neil Armstrong grins after making history as the first person to walk on the moon. Lunar space missions have greatly increased scientists' knowledge of the moon's origins.

Scientist-astronaut Harrison Schmitt of the *Apollo 17* mission bounces over to a selected site to gather moon rocks. Studies of lunar rock samples retrieved by the astronauts have spawned new theories about the moon's origins.

question in the 1800s when sophisticated tools for studying the moon began to be developed. Four popular theories have been proposed and debated since that time.

The sister theory: In 1827 Pierre-Simon de Laplace, a French astronomer and mathematician, proposed the theory that the earth and moon were formed together as companions. If this were true, the earth and the moon would be made of the same materials. For example, the earth's crust and the moon's crust would contain the same amounts of iron. Study of the moon rocks has shown that they do not. Scientists have discovered that although the moon and the earth are made of similar elements, the moon does not have some important metals that the earth has, such as nickel, zinc, and gold.

The daughter theory: In 1878 British mathematician and astronomer Sir George Darwin suggested that the moon was once part of the earth and was thrown off at a time when the earth spun much faster than it does today. Again, more recent research shows that this theory cannot be true. In addition to the two bodies being made of different materials, scientists know that the earth has never spun as fast as it would have had to in order to divide itself. It would have had to spin so fast that an earth day would be condensed into just 2.6 hours!

In 1882 English physicist Osmond Fischer proposed a variation on this theory. He suggested that when the earth was young and still molten, more than 4.6 billion years ago, the gravitational pull of the sun ripped off part of the molten material. This torn-off portion became the moon. The place where the moon had been became the Pacific Ocean. Today scientists know that the Pacific Basin was formed much more recently than 4.6 billion years ago.

Formed Elsewhere in Space?

The pick-up theory: In the 1960s a popular theory was that the moon was formed elsewhere in space and was trapped by the earth's gravity. Most scientists no longer consider this theory to be probable. A wandering satellite, they say, would have had to approach the earth at exactly the right angle, a highly improbable event. If not, it would have bypassed earth's gravitational field entirely or would have crashed violently to the earth's surface.

The impact theory: In the mid-1970s A.G.W. Cameron, professor of astronomy at Harvard University Observatory, and his colleague William Ward proposed the impact theory. They believed the moon was formed when a giant meteor about the size of the planet Mars hit the newly formed earth at about twenty-five hundred miles per hour. This collision tore out a huge chunk of surface matter that eventually formed into the moon. Sophisticated computer models as well as the research done on moon rocks indicate to many scientists that this theory is the most likely explanation for how the moon got into the sky.

Scientists who support this theory explain that although the moon and earth originally came from the same celestial body, because of when and how the meteor smashed into the earth, they are not composed of the same materials. Although the meteor struck soon after the earth was born, the earth's heavy metals such as uranium and plutonium, had already sunk deep within its core. The matter that flew into space and formed the moon was made of lighter materials, such as aluminum, magnesium, and calcium.

Why Does the Moon Have Pockmarks?

While the astronauts moved about the surface of the moon picking up rocks, they were able to take a closer look at something else that has captured the imaginations of people on earth for centuries: moon craters. Without telescopes to help them see the moon's surface clearly, early people imagined many interesting causes for the shadows on the moon.

Man-in-the-moon stories originated thousands of years ago when people looked up at the night sky and imagined human forms in the shadows on the moon. They began to believe that someone lived on the moon. In fact, the word crater comes from the Irish word *cratur*, which means "creature." Different cultures told different stories, and soon these myths became reality to generations of people.

German lore has it that an old man went into the woods one Sunday to chop wood. As he was walking home with a large load on his back, he met a younger man who stopped him.

"Do you know that this is Sunday on earth, when all must rest from their labors?" the young man asked.

"Sunday on earth or Monday in heaven, it's all one to me," replied the old man, shrugging.

NASA scientists create a jigsaw-puzzle-like map from dozens of photos of the lunar surface. The photos were taken by the *Lunar Orbiter IV*. Studying these close-range photographs helps scientists learn more about the moon.

"As you value not Sunday on earth, yours shall be a perpetual moon-day [Monday] in heaven," said the young man. "You shall stand for eternity in the moon, a warning for all sabbath breakers!"

With that, the young man vanished and the old woodcutter was whisked to the moon, where to this day people on earth see him carrying his burden.

The Frisians, the most ancient German tribe, believed the man in the moon was a thief who stole cabbages from his neighbor's garden on Christmas Eve. When people saw him trying to sneak away, they "wished" him to the moon, where he remained in shame, holding a cabbage for eternity so that everyone could know of his crime.

In some parts of Germany during the Middle Ages (approximately 600 to 1400), people believed that both a man and a woman inhabited the moon as punishment for wrongs they had done. The man had thrown thorns along the path to church, preventing

A seal depicts the medieval German folk tale of a man carrying sticks on the moon. He was banished there for preventing worshipers from getting to church by strewing thorns in their path. The Latin inscription reads, "I will teach you, Walter, why I carry thorns on the moon."

worshipers from entering on Sunday, and the woman had made butter on the sabbath. Similar myths were told in other areas throughout Europe, with different details. In some, the man in the moon was said to be stealing sheep, in others, he was stealing willow boughs.

As this photograph taken from *Apollo 8* reveals, the spots on the moon are not mythical inhabitants but huge craters caused by meteors striking its surface.

These myths, probably encouraged by some religious orders, not only explained the moon's shadows but also served to remind people about the importance of honoring holy days and the commands of the Church. Alexander Neckam, a twelfth-century English poet and scholar, wrote:

The Rustic in the moon,
Whose burden weighs him down,
This changeless truth reveals,
He profits not who steals.

Not all man-in-the-moon myths were created to teach people a religious lesson. For instance, the ancient Greeks believed moon spots were islands of paradise where everyone lived in friendship after they died; the Malays thought the spots were a hunchbacked man sitting under a banyan tree; the Eskimos thought the moon held a house covered with animal skins and guarded by walruses; and the Creek tribe of North America thought the moon was inhabited by a man and a dog.

In Greenland, myth has it that the moon and the sun began as two mortals, a boy named Anninga, and his sister, Malina. One night they were playing outside with their friends. When Anninga began to tease his sister, she covered her hands with soot from a lamp and smeared his face with it. Her brother began to chase her, so she flew high into the sky and became the sun. Anninga jumped after her, but he could not climb as high, so he became the moon—with the soot still on his face. That is why, Greenlanders say, the moon has shadows.

Rabbits on the Moon

Asian, African, Indian, English, and South American cultures all have myths in which the shadows on the moon have to do with a rabbit. In Sanskrit, an ancient language of India, the moon is called Sasankra, which means "hare mark" or "spot." Some mythologists—people who study the origins of myths—believe the rabbit is associated with the moon because the animal's gestation period is thirty days, the same length as the moon's cycle.

A beautiful Buddhist moon-rabbit myth is the story of a hare, a monkey, a fox, and a coot (a species of water bird) who live in the wilderness together and promise that they will not kill any living thing. The god Sakkria decides to test their sincerity. He comes to earth in the form of a Brahman (a priest) and begs the monkey for food. The monkey brings him mangoes. Next the Brahman asks the coot for food, and the bird brings him fish left on a

The hare in the moon. Many cultures from all over the world have a myth about a rabbit or hare living on the moon. The origin of this connection between the moon and rabbits may be that a rabbit's gestation cycle is about thirty days, the same as the lunar cycle.

riverbank by a fisherman. The fox brings the Brahman a pot of milk forgotten by the goatherd. Finally, the Brahman asks the hare to bring him food.

"I eat nothing but grass," the hare says, "and that will be of no use to you." The Brahman decides to test the hare. "Why not give me your own flesh, a true sacrifice?" he asks. The Brahman makes a fire, and the hare—bravely and dutifully—leaps into it. Just as the hare is about to touch the hot flames, the Brahman extinguishes the fire and reappears in his true form as the god Sakkria. Then he takes the hare in his arms and brings him to the moon so that living things throughout the world will see him for all eternity and know of his bravery and integrity.

The Moon Lake

Another Asian rabbit-moon myth tells of a herd of elephants wandering through the forest in search of water. Finally they come upon a huge body of water called the moon lake. As they walk to the water to drink, they trample large numbers of rabbits that live nearby, hurting many of them and even killing a few.

When the elephants finally leave for a while, the rabbits meet to discuss what to do when the elephants return. One brave rabbit promises to get rid of the elephants. He visits the elephant king and tells him that he is the rabbit that lives in the moon. "The moon wants me to tell you that if you and your elephants drink again from the lake, he will no longer provide you with night, and you will be burned up by perpetual sunlight."

The elephant goes to the lake and sees the moon's reflection in the water. As he looks, his long trunk falls into the water, causing the reflection to ripple. The elephant thinks the moon is shaking because it is enraged, so he apologizes and walks rapidly away forever.

Some native villagers in South America believe a baby lives on the moon. Legend has it that the

"For now, the giant impact theory offers the best account of lunar origin, that the moon was born in one of the most violent catastrophes in solar system history."

William K. Hartmann, *Natural History*, November 1989

"One thing that bothers me about the [impact] theory is that you must have available for the collision a Mars-sized body very late in the formation of the solar system, and I don't believe there are any good models that would produce such a body so late."

John Wasson, astronomer

baby was the son of a tribal chief. The baby was ignored by his mother when he cried out one night for her to give him a drink of water. The moon came down with a pot of water and, after the baby drank his fill, carried him through a secret underground passage out of town and up into heaven. The baby remains there today and has all the water he wants.

Science Replaces Myth

In 1609 ideas about the moon's surface changed forever. In that year, the Italian astronomer Galileo Galilei turned a recent invention—the telescope—on the moon. For the first time in history, people could see what the moon was really like. Galileo peered through his telescope and discovered craters,

In the seventeenth century Italian astronomer Galileo Galilei used the newly invented telescope to dispel long-accepted myths about the moon, sun, and other planets.

mountains, and dark areas that he called *maria*—the Latin word for "seas"—because he believed they were filled with water.

"The surface of the moon is not perfectly smooth," Galileo wrote. "It is uneven, full of bumps and hollows, just like the surface of the earth itself, which is varied everywhere by lofty mountains and deep valleys."

Early Theories About Craters

Earlier in this century, scientists had several theories about how the moon's craters were formed. One was that the craters were ancient coral atolls that had formed when the moon's seas were filled with water. When the astronauts brought back moon rocks from their space expedition in 1969, scientists proved that no water ever filled these seas. The marias were most likely filled, not with coral, but with hot lava. It could have come either from volcanoes or from the moon's core, broken through when meteorites violently struck the surface.

A second theory was that craters were formed when small, natural satellites that once orbited the moon crash-landed on the lunar surface. People who believed this theory thought the satellites were chunks of rocks, possibly pieces of the moon that flicked off its surface as it formed. They explained that the satellites were trapped in the moon's orbit by its gravitational pull. Eventually the rocks got close enough to the moon to get sucked into a collision. Today the moon has no natural satellites orbiting it, and there is no hard evidence that the moon ever had any moons of its own.

A third theory was that the craters were made of ice. The people who believed this did not know that on the moon the temperature reaches 250 degrees Fahrenheit—hot enough to melt an iceberg, if icebergs were ever there!

A fourth theory was that the moon was inhabited at one time, but that the lunar citizens destroyed

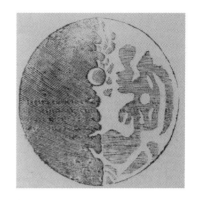

Galileo drew this sketch showing the irregular patterns that he saw on the moon's surface.

Visitors to the Smithsonian Institution in Washington, D.C., are fascinated by a moon rock specimen on display. In the past, moon rocks were kept in a sterile environment because no one knew if they contained harmful organisms.

each other as well as all the plants and animal life. The craters supposedly resulted from nuclear explosions.

As scientific instruments have become more sophisticated and precise, researchers have learned more about what the surface and atmosphere of the moon are made of. Most scientists believe that the temperature and atmosphere of the moon could never have allowed human life to exist.

Billions of craters dimple the moon's landscape. Some craters are so big—several hundred miles wide—that they have little craters inside them. Today most scientists believe that many of the craters were formed by the impact of meteorites and that others were formed by volcanoes. Some craters, such as Tycho, formed about 109 million years ago,

and Copernicus, formed about 810 million years ago, have rays extending from their centers, making them resemble rocky sunbursts. The rays, say scientists, are made of material that blasted out of the craters formed when a meteor hit.

Unanswered Questions Remain

Earth's closest "relative" in space—the moon—has been an object of poetry and prose for thousands of years. In the last few hundred, researchers have developed and used scientific methods in hopes of discovering how the moon and the earth—in fact, all the cosmos—were formed. Lunar exploration has helped scientists rule out many myths and early theories about the moon's formation and its makeup. In 1969 the moon rocks brought back to earth by the astronauts were kept in a sterile environment because no one knew if they contained organisms that would harm people or other living things on earth. They did not. In fact, the moon rocks show that no life of any kind has ever existed on the moon. It is truly a lifeless world.

Or is it?

As good as scientific instruments are today, they have not been able to answer all questions absolutely. That is why some scientists think we should not decide such questions as whether there is life on the moon until all of the moon has been explored and we learn more about how the cosmos came to be.

A 1967 photo of the lunar surface taken at a distance of 135 miles by *Lunar Orbiter V* shows that the moon is nothing but a desolate, lifeless orb.

Four

How Did the Moon Affect People's Daily Lives?

Before the invention of timepieces such as clocks and watches, people relied on nature to determine the passage of time. They saw patterns in the natural world that could help them plan their lives. The sun, the moon, and the seasons all went through regular cycles. People discovered that by keeping records of these cycles, they could begin to plan certain events in their lives. They could plan when to plant and harvest, for example. They could anticipate when certain animals would be plentiful to hunt. They could figure out how much time passed between one rainy season and the next.

At first people kept crude records of days, months, seasons, and years by making simple marks on stones and bone. Later they developed sophisticated timepieces and calendars.

Moon Bones

Some of the earliest time records archaeologists have found are bits of engraved bones that scholars think are lunar calendars. The earliest examples date back about thirty thousand years. Bits of bone found in central Africa and in caves in France have incised marks that seem to reflect a record of the moon's movement. The cluster of marks on a bone looks

(Opposite page) A harvest moon rises in all its arresting magnificence. Does this yearly optical illusion really affect people's lives?

"The moon is the epitome of continuous time reckoning, for its behavior suggests both continuity and duration; yet its changing aspects make it nature's ideal event marker as it exhibits noticeable differences from night to night."

Anthony Aveni, *Empires of Time: Calendars, Clocks, and Cultures*

"The moon's cycle is the backbone, the fundamental structure, of many traditional calendars, but we don't really know that the neolithic and Bronze Age peoples of northwestern Europe calibrated time in terms of the moon."

E.C. Krupp, *Echoes of the Ancient Skies: The Astronomy of Lost Civilizations*

like a series of commas. The first fourteen or fifteen commas are curved in the same direction along the edge of the bone. Then there is a longer, straight line, followed by another series of fourteen or fifteen commas curved in the opposite direction. Alexander Marshack, the American who studied the marks, believes the commas correspond to the number of days in the waxing and waning moons. The line in the middle could indicate the full moon, he believes.

Most anthropologists agree with Marshack, but some scientists do not think Ice Age people had the intelligence to think up such a way to keep track of time. Primitive people, they say, lived day-to-day existences and did not think about next month or next year. "Some . . . say that permanent calendar keeping is not consistent with what we know about the level of intelligence of these early people," writes author Anthony Aveni. "Counting days would have been a concept . . . too abstract for them to fathom." People such as Aveni think the grooves are more likely marks left by a hunter sharpening a knife or by someone counting something.

Presa de la Mula

Scientists are more certain about other lunar calendars found in a variety of cultures. In northwest Mexico, for example, stone patterns similar to those on the bones studied by Marshack have been dated at about four thousand to five thousand years old. One stone, the Presa de la Mula, tallies seven lunar months. The stone is a one-meter by three-meter slab that can be reached only by climbing to the top of a cliff. The slab has dot-and-line patterns that seem to measure approximate lunar months of twenty-seven to thirty days each. Because these stone slabs were found next to engraved lists of weapons and animal kills, some anthropologists believe the tribes who lived in that area used a seven-month calendar to mark the hunting and planting seasons.

Several early civilizations used observatories to

detect the patterns of the moon, stars, and sun. Early people were very selective about where they set up their observatories. They looked for places that gave them the best view of the sky and where the stones they carefully arranged to mark the passage of time would not be disturbed.

Ancient people often used graves as astronomical observatories. It was very dark at the burial grounds and the area was not disturbed by people walking over it throughout the day.

One kind of grave frequently used as a sky observatory was a "passage grave." A passage grave is a burial place at the end of a passage, usually underground or under the shelter of carefully erected rocks. Many of these graves have been found in Europe, Ireland, and Great Britain.

Newgrange

In eastern Ireland, a large, ancient cemetery lies where the river Boyne turns to meet the sea. It is the site of Newgrange, one of the most famous passage graves, and of several other graves. Newgrange is a large, round mound made of rock and pebbles. Inside the mound is a long passage that ends in a twelve-foot-high group of rooms resembling a cross. A decorative stone once blocked the entry to the sixty-two-foot-long passage. During the full moon at the winter solstice (the shortest day of the year), a window box built into the wall above the entrance allows a thin moon beam to strike the far wall of the end room.

The people who lived here once called the moon the White Goddess, and at Newgrange its presence was marked with white quartzite, engraved spirals, concentric circles, and chevrons. Sunlight entering the grave illuminates these goddess markings. Scholars believe ancient people used this grave to observe the celestial bodies, record their passage, and plan their year.

While Newgrange is one of the most famous

passage-grave observatories, many other sites were also used to plot the movement of the moon. For instance, a passage mound in Brittany, France, called Gavrinis, is aligned to the moon, and engravings in the passage celebrate the moon.

Stonehenge

The most famous of the sacred places and stone calendars is Stonehenge, which was erected by ancient Britons. Stonehenge, in England's Salisbury Plain, is one of the world's greatest mysteries. Two rings of stone slabs, several solitary slabs, and slabs that form doorways were used by ancient people to define sacred spaces. Stonehenge is the most magnificient of the stone circles found in the British Isles.

Lunar and solar events such as eclipses could be predicted by viewing the alignment of certain stones. The ability to predict such important events would give great power to the interpreter—often a priest of an ancient religion.

The entire structure of Stonehenge is believed to have originally been dedicated to the Mother Goddess, or moon. Markers show the phases of the moon, and a pair of ox horns—a moon fertility symbol—were dug up in the central area of the monument.

In the book *Origins of the Sacred,* author Anne Bancroft says Stonehenge represented the ultimate honor bestowed upon the lunar and solar deities. "Undoubtedly the moon was a goddess, the sun almost certainly a deity too, and very likely the larger stars and planets were endowed with deity status," she says. "It would have been a tremendous act of homage to build [Stonehenge] in such a way that seen from the sky it would be more significant than seen from the ground."

Stonehenge changed over time from a place of moon worship into a solar observatory. "Here Druid priestesses or priests later calculated the cycles of

the moon, sun, and stars in order to predict seasonal phases and natural events and to provide a center of worship of the natural order," writes author Barbara G. Walker. The predictions of the priests and priestesses probably guided people's farming and other plans.

Not all scholars believe Stonehenge was used as an observatory. Some say Neolithic farmers, who lived during the early Bronze Age, would not have been interested in keeping such an exact account of time. They suggest that the three hundred stone circles in the British Isles (including Stonehenge) and northern France may have been used as gathering places where ceremonies and rituals were performed for the rulers of the tribes. Stonehenge may have been the headquarters where the supreme chief of the tribe was honored in ceremonies.

Still others are not sure how Stonehenge was used. "The moon's cycle is the backbone, the fun-

Native Americans plant food for the coming year. Early peoples lived their lives in rhythm with nature. The phases of the moon marked that rhythm.

damental structure of many traditional calendars," says writer and astronomer E.C. Krupp, "but we don't really know that the Neolithic and Bronze Age peoples of northwestern Europe calibrated time in terms of the moon."

The scientific community is divided on the issue of how ancient people might have used places like Stonehenge and Presa de la Mula. Generally, astronomers are more likely to think these places were used to track the movement of the sun, moon, and stars. Anthropologists, on the other hand, are more apt to believe that these places were used for tribal rituals. Experts are continuing to conduct excavations around the world. One of them may uncover artifacts that will give us the answer.

You Can Count on It!

The word *month* comes from the Old English word for *moon*. Its usc comes from the practice of counting time's passage by the number of days between the occurrences of a particular phase of the

Mysterious Stonehenge on Britain's Salisbury Plain was probably built to observe the movement of the stars, planets, sun, and moon. Its stones were precisely set to mark the yearly journey of the sun from solstice to solstice.

moon. It takes about a month for the moon to move around the earth—about a month between one full moon and the next and between one new moon and the next. Different cultures used different phases as the starting point for their months. The month was perhaps the first long-range time measurement for ancient people.

With careful observation, astronomers eventually were able to be more precise in their measurements of the moon's passage. They discovered that a lunar month, also called a synodic month, is actually twenty-nine-and-a-half days.

As early people continued to observe nature, those in many parts of the world discovered that it follows a regular pattern of four seasons. This pattern eventually became known as a year.

Lunar Time Versus Solar Time

The seasons are determined by the earth's position in relation to the sun. Inconveniently, lunar time and solar time do not match. For instance, the lunar day is fifty minutes longer than the solar day. A solar day (determined by the time it takes the earth to rotate once on its axis) is almost exactly twenty-four hours, but a lunar day is twenty-four hours and fifty minutes. So a lunar-timed event occurring at 8 A.M. today will occur at 8:50 A.M. tomorrow.

To add to the confusion, a year has thirteen lunar months that do not exactly coordinate with the four seasons. So those who used a lunar calendar to count the passage of time eventually found themselves out of phase with the sun-caused seasons. The lunar calendar moves further and further out of phase with the sun each month.

Many civilizations used to have lunar calendars, but in the sixteenth century, people began to switch to a solar-based calendar. It was a more accurate way to count the days and months in a year. Today just about everyone uses the calendar we use—the

"Here [at Stonehenge] Druidic priestesses or priests later calculated the cycles of the moon, sun, and stars in order to predict seasonal phases and natural events and to provide a center of worship of the natural order."

Barbara G. Walker, *The Woman's Dictionary of Symbols and Sacred Objects*

"Critics . . . do not believe that precise observation of the moon was of interest in the Early Bronze Age."

E.C. Krupp, *Echoes of the Ancient Skies: The Astronomy of Lost Civilizations*

Gregorian calendar—for business and ordinary activities. Some cultures use other calendars for religious and ceremonial purposes.

The Gregorian calendar is a solar calendar. It was established by Pope Gregory XIII in 1582. The rise of Christianity required a fixed calendar so that feasts such as Easter could be predicted. Pope Gregory and a small group of astronomers refined the solar-based calendar established by Julius Caesar in the first century B.C. The Gregorian calendar is based on a 365-day year and closely matches the solar cycle. Non-Catholic countries such as England did not adopt the Gregorian calendar at first.

Different Places, Different Years

People who use lunar calendars perform intercalation—adding extra days or entire months to make the lunar calendar even with the solar year.

Here are some examples of societies that have used lunar calendars:

• The Chinese calendar is the oldest calendar and may be more than forty-five hundred years old. It is made up of twelve lunar months of twenty-nine

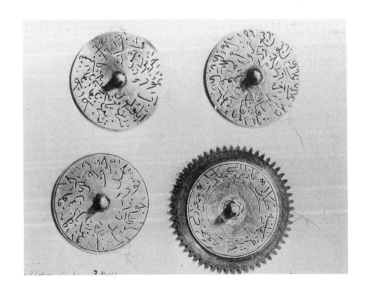

Because time is marked by cycles, calendars were conceived in the shape of a wheel. This collection of ancient Persian calendars includes (clockwise from top left) a solar calendar noting Christian holy days, a lunar calendar marking Muslim holy days, a zodiac, or star calendar, and a calendar marking the days of the week.

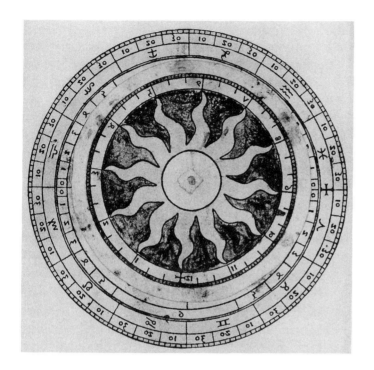

A fifteenth-century calendar incorporates the zodiac as well as the yearly cycle of the sun and the moon. These popular and useful circular calendars were called *volvelles*.

or thirty days each. It counts out a sixty-year cycle, made up of five twelve-year cycles. Each of the twelve years is named after an animal: Rat, Ox, Tiger, Hare, Dragon, Snake, Horse, Sheep, Monkey, Cock, Dog, Pig. The Chinese calendar is still used today.

• The ancient Babylonian calendar, from 500 B.C., was based on a lunar month that began when the first crescent was visible. The Babylonians recognized twelve months of twenty-nine or thirty days and added extra months so that the lunar calendar and solar year came out even every nineteen years.

The Babylonians called the day of the full moon *sapaatu*—the time of "heart rest," when the moon is full and rests from its constant waxing and waning for one day each month. It was important to keep track of when these full moons would occur, since the Babylonians believed it was unlucky to do anything on sapaatu. When the Hebrews were enslaved by the Babylonians, they probably adopted the idea of sapaatu and created the Hebrew sabbath day of rest. The Hebrews, however, took the idea one step further and applied the sabbath to the days of the new and quarter moons. That is why there is one sabbath day a week.

• The ancient Egyptians based their calendar on the annual flooding of the Nile River. The first month of the year occurred on the new moon after the Nile flooded. The year consisted of twelve months, the first eleven with thirty days, the last one with thirty-five days. Eventually, they began to use a solar calendar. The Egyptians were the first civilization to use a 365-day year.

• The Jewish calendar still uses a nineteen-year cycle. Each month in the Jewish calendar begins with the sighting of the crescent moon. Twelve of the nineteen years have twelve months. The other seven years have thirteen. This helps keep the moon-based calendar in line with the solar year.

• The Muslim calendar is also a lunar calendar and is made up of a thirty-three-year cycle of twenty-nine- or thirty-day months. The first year of the Muslim calendar is A.D. 622 on our calendar. This was the year Muhammad, the founder of the Muslim religion, Islam, left the city of Mecca.

• The Hindu calendar appeared about three thousand years ago. It is composed of twelve months of twenty-seven or twenty-eight days each. Every sixty months an extra month is added to keep pace with the solar year.

• In the nineteenth century the midwestern Winnebago tribe followed a sophisticated lunar calendar to organize hunting, planting, and festivals. A four-and-a-half-foot-long stick recorded the moon's cycles for two lunar years. The months varied from twenty-eight to thirty-two days each. Every three years the Winnebago added an extra

The prophet Muhammad preaching at Mecca. The Muslim calendar, based on the lunar cycle, begins with the year Muhammad was forced to flee Mecca—A.D. 622.

In 45 B.C. Julius Caesar added extra days to the Roman lunar calendar so that it would keep pace with the sun's yearly cycle. The Julian calendar was used in Europe from Caesar's time until A.D. 1582.

month to bring the lunar calendar in step with the solar year.

• The Roman calendar was originally a lunar calendar. Julius Caesar added extra days so that the calendar would keep pace with the sun. The Julian calendar became the norm throughout much of the Western world from 45 B.C. until A.D. 1582, when Pope Gregory developed his solar calendar.

Month Names That Reflect Nature

Since the days of the cave dwellers, people have made a connection between the moon, the changing seasons, and the passage of time. The cycles of the moon have helped farmers to know when to plant and harvest crops and sailors and fishermen to know when to set sail across the ocean. The names given to the months by Native Americans and by early American colonists show these connections:

January	Colonial American	Winter Moon
	Algonquin	Wolf Moon
	Nez Percé	Cold Weather Moon
	Haida	Younger Moon
February	Colonial American	Trapper's Moon
	Kutenai	Black Bear moon
	Taos	Elder Moon
	Zuni	No Snow on Trails Moon
March	Colonial American	Fish Moon
	Algonquin	Crow Moon
	Nez Percé	Flower Time Moon
	Oto	Big Clouds Moon
April	Colonial American	Planter's Moon
	Lakota Sioux	Moon of Grass Appearing
	Illinois	Do Nothing Moon
	Oto	Little Frogs Croak Moon
May	Colonial American	Milk Moon
	Cheyenne	Time When the Horses Get Fat Moon
	Taos	Corn Planting Moon
June	Colonial American	Rose Moon
	Algonquin	Strawberry Moon
	Nez Percé	Salmon Fishing Time Moon
	San Juan	Leaf Dark Moon
July	Colonial American	Hay Moon
	Lakota Sioux	Moon When the Cherries Are Ripe
	Pima	Moon of the Giant Cactus
	Haida	Killer Whale Moon

August	Colonial American	Woodcutter's Moon
	Cherokee	Moon of the New Ripened Corn
	Haida	Collect Food for the Winter Moon
	San Juan	Wheat Cut Moon
September	Colonial American	Harvest Moon
	Cheyenne	Cool Moon
	Oto	Spider Web on the Ground at Dawn Moon
	San Juan	Leaf Fall Moon
October	Colonial American	Hunter's Moon
	Wisham	Travel in Canoes Moon
	Kutenai	Falling River Moon
	San Juan	Leaf Fall Moon
November	Colonial American	Beaver Moon
	Lakota Sioux	Moon of the Falling Leaves
	Oto	Every Buck Loses His Horns Moon
	Nez Percé	Autumn Time Moon
December	Colonial American	Christmas Moon
	Cheyenne	Big Freezing Moon
	Oto	Cold Month Moon
	Lakota Sioux	Moon of the Popping Trees

Five

Does the Moon Cause Madness?

Does the moon make people insane? Do normal people turn into fierce werewolves in the light of the full moon? Does crime increase when the moon shines brightly? The answers depend on which research studies people look at, since research has supported both "Yes" and "No" answers to these questions.

Werewolves

Stories of people becoming wolves appear in just about every culture. For example, the ancient Romans believed the goddess Diana could transform anyone who offended her into a werewolf. Navajos believed werewolves were night-roaming ghouls that rustled sheep, stole jewelry, and cannibalized unwary passersby.

Many societies that have believed in werewolves believed the condition was punishment by the gods to humans who made them angry. One Greek legend, for example, tells the tale of a man named Lycaon, who tried to trick the god Zeus. Zeus became so angry that he turned Lycaon into a wolf. Lycaon's jaws slathered with foam and he thirsted for blood. His clothes turned into coarse fur and his eyes became wild. He raged among the

flocks, slaughtering sheep.

In North America prehistoric people did live among wolves and roam the fields. These hunters competed with wolves for game and developed a healthy respect for the wolf as a cunning and efficient animal hunter. In fact, medicine people from some tribes of Native Americans so admired the hunting skills of wolves that they actually wanted to become wolves themselves! They dressed in wolf skins and acted out wolflike behavior to bring the skill of the wolf to the hunters of their tribes.

Werewolves and the Moon

Since the days of the early Greeks and Romans, just about every culture has noted the relationship between werewolves and the full moon. One example is a classic Greek tale in the book *Satyricon*. In that story, a slave named Niceros decides to walk five miles to his girlfriend's house. Because it is late

An old German woodcut depicts a werewolf attacking a villager. Many cultures include lore about humans who become wolves under the light of the full moon.

at night, he asks a soldier to walk with him. In the bright light of the full moon they come to a graveyard. The soldier steps away to examine the tombstones. When Niceros looks back a short time later, he sees that the soldier has taken off his clothes and poured water in a circle around them. Suddenly, the soldier turns into a wolf and runs away. Petronius, the author of the story, explains that the water protected the soldier's clothes so that he could regain his human form when he returned from his wanderings as a wolf.

Sabine Baring-Gould was a nineteenth-century English clergyman, archaeologist, folklorist, novelist, and composer. He wrote about the French people's belief that certain individuals are destined to become werewolves:

> They are transformed into wolves at full moon. The desire to run comes upon them at night. They leave their beds, jump out of a window, and plunge into a fountain. After the bath, they come out covered with fur, walking on all fours, and commence a raid over fields and meadows, through woods and villages, biting all beasts and human beings that come their way. At the approach of dawn, they return to the spring, plunge into it, lose their furry skins, and regain their deserted beds.

Tradition in Sicily, Italy, has it that a child conceived on a new moon will become a werewolf. According to writer Summers Montague, in Palermo, Italy, citizens say that as the moon becomes full, the werewolf "is seized with fearful writhings and pangs, after which his limbs quiver and contract horribly, he howls and rushes off on all fours, shunning the light."

Lycanthropy

From the time of the Roman Empire to today, physicians and psychologists have studied reports of people turning into wolves. In fact, scientists

"Even a man who is pure in heart
And says his prayers by night,
Can become a wolf when the wolfsbane blooms
And the autumn moon is bright."

Curt Siodmak, *The Wolf Man*

"I believe that the so-called werewolves of the past may, at least in the majority of instances, have been suffering from congenital porphyria. The evidence for this lies in the remarkable relation between the symptoms of this rare disease and the many accounts of werewolves that have come down to us."

Lee Illis, *On Porphyria and the Aetiology of Werewolves*

came up with a medical name for becoming a were-wolf—*lycanthropy*, which comes from the legend of Lycaon.

In the sixteenth century doctors thought lycanthropy was caused by the devil, who turned unsuspecting people into raving animals. "The devil can really and materially metamorphose the body of a man into that of an animal and thereby cause the sickness," said Jean Bodin, a sixteenth-century French physician.

Thirty thousand cases of lycanthropy were reported in Europe during the sixteenth century. Anyone who looked even vaguely wolfish—who had a long, narrow face or long, sharp canine teeth—was accused of being a werewolf. The search for proof involved grisly examinations. Often the unfortunate accused person had the skin on his or her back torn off so examiners could look for wolf fur hidden underneath. Frequently people confessed to being werewolves just to end the torture. Accused werewolves were often burned at the stake.

Some people who believed themselves to be werewolves locked themselves up at the time of the full moon to keep from going out and attacking innocent people. Less-sensitive monsters took to the fields and city streets, looking for sheep or people to slaughter. Werewolves were thought to frequent remote places, such as cow pastures and cemeteries. There they could attack their victims without being seen by others.

Spells and Charms

People did not have much protection from werewolves, but there were a few good-luck spells to chant and some charms to carry or wear that supposedly kept werewolves away. A classic method was to confront the beast with the sign of the cross. In Italy, even today, some babies born at the full moon are branded with a cross on their necks so that they will not turn into werewolves as adults.

Another way people thought they could keep werewolves at bay was to draw three drops of blood from the beast—if anyone dared to get close enough to do it! After guns came into vogue, people believed they could kill werewolves with silver bullets. (Silver is the color of the moon, which gives the werewolf life.)

Modern Werewolves

If you think werewolf stories come only from the past, think again. "Lycanthropy is a rare phenomenon, but it does exist," wrote Harvey Rosenstock and Kenneth Vincent in an article published in the *American Journal of Psychiatry* in 1977. Here are some modern tales of lycanthropy:

• In 1949 Roman police supposedly found a werewolf in the bushes of a Roman garden. A young man, covered in mud, was digging in the ground

A series of Old English woodcuts depicts the life, arrest, condemnation, and execution of sorcerer Peter Stump, who took the shape of a wolf and terrorized a medieval village. To ensure Stump's destruction, his execution included plucking out his heart and beheading, then burning, his corpse.

with his long fingernails and was howling at the moon. When taken to a local hospital and calmed down, he claimed this behavior occurred regularly during the full moon.

• In the 1960s an article published in a scientific journal reported the case of a Frenchman who claimed he was a werewolf. The man believed that his teeth grew into fangs, his feet changed into wolf feet, and wolf hair covered his body. He also claimed that he craved raw meat.

• The *Canadian Psychiatric Association Journal* reported the case of "Mr. W" in an article published in 1975. Mr. W was a farmer who allowed his facial hair to grow long, as if it were fur. He slept in cemeteries and howled at the full moon. Mr. W claimed to be a werewolf.

Common features of werewolves have been reported in all cultures: The person's palms become hairy, hands curve like talons, nails grow into claws, facial and head hair grow into a mane, eyes redden and glow like a cat's, the body becomes furry, a rash appears on the chest, toes become deformed and calloused, and skin becomes frayed and coarse. Headaches, labored breathing, and uncontrollable foaming at the mouth are also considered to be characteristics of lycanthropy.

Because the same general description of people turning into werewolves has appeared in cultures throughout the world for hundreds of years, some people believe these stories must be true. However, other people insist that werewolves are nothing but silly superstition. Truth or fiction? Perhaps there is a third explanation.

Porphyria

Perhaps people do not really turn into wolves. Maybe they suffer from a medical condition that causes them to look and act wolflike. That theory is what Dr. Lee Illis of Hampshire, England, reported to the Royal Society of Medicine in 1963. He de-

scribed a little-known, medically recognized disease called porphyria—a condition so rare that only eighty cases had ever been reported.

Dr. Illis noted that the symptoms of lycanthropy closely match the medically documented symptoms of porphyria. For instance, porphyria sores make the sufferer's skin extremely sensitive to touch and light. Porphyria victims do not want to shave their hair or go out into the sunlight because it is too painful, so they wait until dark to venture outside.

Epilepsy, a disorder of the nervous system, sometimes accompanies porphyria. It may be the true medical explanation for some of the more grotesque symptoms of lycanthropy. For example, during an epileptic seizure, people lose control of their body movements. They may thrash about, foam at the mouth, and make loud groaning and

Werewolves attack a man foolish enough to be out late at night during a full moon. The illustration is from Sabine Baring-Gould's *Book of Werewolves.*

growling noises. Before doctors learned that epilepsy was a disease, people were frightened by such sudden and dramatic outbursts.

It is not difficult to imagine how someone with the symptoms caused by porphyria could be thought to be a werewolf! Notes author Basil Cooper,

> The wandering about at night, which the victim of porphyria would find more bearable than exposure to daylight; the . . . lesions to the skin of the face and the hands, typical of the werewolf who had been bitten by wild animals; and possible nervous manifestations; all would have been enough, in medieval times, to condemn such a poor wretch to the execution block as a proven werewolf.

As with other symptoms of porphyria and lycanthropy, the onset of epilepsy is believed by some people to be influenced by the moon. The relationship between the disease we now call epilepsy and the moon is even mentioned in the Bible. For example, the Latin Vulgate Bible tells the story of a man who takes his son to Jesus to be cured of (epileptic) seizures. The boy is described as *lunaticus* (moonstruck). And the Old Testament warns that people who stand naked in front of a shining light such as the full moon may get seizures.

Historically, some people believed that those who had the illness were being punished for offending the moon deity. They also believed that seizures became worse as the moon waxed and that afflicted persons were most violent at the full moon.

Murder, Mayhem, and Madness

Today, the symptoms of epilepsy and porphyria can be controlled with medication. But Dr. Illis's research did not put to rest the idea that werewolves exist. One reason may be that Dr. Illis's medical explanation is not as exciting and mysterious as the belief that people turn into wolves.

The belief that the moon—especially the full

"It's true . . . some people get loonier than others when the moon is full."

Newspaper columnist Ann Landers, August 27, 1984

"Phases of the moon accounted for no more than $\frac{3}{100}$ of 1 percent of the . . . activities usually termed *lunacy*."

I.W. Kelly, James Rotton, and Roger Culver, *Skeptical Inquirer*, Winter 1985-86

moon—makes people insane is also an ancient idea. The Latin word for "moon" is *luna*, and Luna is the Roman goddess of the moon. *Luna* is also the source of the word *lunacy* (madness). Many primitive people believed that the moon was an evil deity who could drive people insane if they stared at it or slept in its full light. Even highly respected philosophers and writers noted the effects of the moon on people's sanity: "One who is seized with terror, fright, and madness during the night is being visited by the goddess of the moon," said the physician Hippocrates of ancient Greece. And Shakespeare wrote of moon madness in his play *Othello*:

> It is the very error of the moon;
> She come more near the earth than she was wont,
> And makes men mad.

Many Examples

Here are some other examples of old beliefs about the moon's connection to madness and crime:

• Bedouins, wandering tribes of Arabs, believed that staring at the moon would make people mad.

• An old Scandinavian tale, "The Magic Mirror," tells of a king who became a beast at the full moon.

• The ancient Egyptians believed that insanity could be cured if the sufferer ate meatballs made from snake meat in the light of the full moon.

• In 1842 England passed the Lunacy Acts, which defined a lunatic as a demented person who had lucid periods during the first two phases of the moon, then became afflicted with madness during and following the full moon.

• Charles Hyde, an English laborer, took advantage of the Lunacy Acts ten years after they were passed. Hyde committed criminal acts at the new and full moons. When he was brought to trial, he defended himself on the grounds of lunacy—the moon had made him mad. His defense did him no

An illustration from Robert Louis Stevenson's classic tale of human madness, *The Strange Case of Dr. Jekyll and Mr. Hyde.* The character of Hyde was based on a real-life London criminal who blamed his crimes on moon madness.

Leon Trotsky, an important figure in the history of Soviet communism, was assassinated in 1940 during a full moon.

good, however, and Hyde went to jail for his crimes in 1854. (Hyde was the model for the story *The Strange Case of Dr. Jekyll and Mr. Hyde*, written by Robert Louis Stevenson.)

Our own twentieth century has examples of lunar mayhem as well. Consider these grisly events:

• Russian war minister Leon Trotsky was assassinated in 1940 during a full moon.

• The My Lai massacre in Vietnam occurred in 1968 during a full moon.

• The New York serial killer called Son of Sam killed on eight different nights between 1976 and 1978. Five of those nights had either full or new moons.

• In 1974 the Sybionese Liberation Army kidnapped newspaper heiress Patty Hearst during a full moon.

• Sara Moore shot at American president Gerald Ford during a full moon in 1975.

Coincidence?

Is it just a coincidence that all of these crimes and acts of violence happened at the time of a full moon? Some modern-day scientists and professionals who work in hospitals, prisons, and fire departments do not think so. "I have no doubt that the moon has an effect on human behavior," the famous astronomer Carl Sagan has written.

Police officers say more crimes are reported when the moon is full. "There is an increase in the number of assaults and crimes between people at a full moon," observed Harvey Schlossberg, a psychologist and director of the New York Police Department's psychological services unit.

Surveys of hospitals in Oregon and Massachusetts in 1978 showed that admissions to mental hospitals increased 50 percent at the time of the full moon and that psychotic people act more aggressively during a full moon. The surveys included accounts of people tearing up raw meat and running

David Berkowitz (right), known as the Son of Sam killer, killed eight women over a two-year period in the mid-1970s. Most of the murders took place on full or new moons.

wild—not unlike the old tales of werewolf behavior!

A fire chief for the San Francisco fire department said in a 1977 interview with a newspaper reporter that during full moons his department received more calls reporting fires, false alarms, cats stuck in trees, and climbers stranded on cliffs.

Bartenders who have been interviewed on the subject report that people are louder, more aggressive, and seem to get drunk more easily at the time of the full moon.

Studying the Evidence

One scientist who has researched the moon's effects on human behavior is psychiatrist Arnold Lieber. The Miami, Florida, doctor began his research in 1956 by studying murder records for a fifteen-year period in Dade County, Florida. In 1958 he began a study of thirteen years of murders in

Cuyahoga County, Ohio. He looked at a total of almost four thousand cases in these studies. When he compared the dates of murders to the phases of the moon at those times, he discovered that the murders occurred most often around the times of the full moon.

In January 1974 the moon and sun were in a straight line, and the moon was at its perigee—the time when it is its closest to the earth. That created an increased gravitational pull on the earth. Dr. Lieber predicted that the extra pull and a full moon combined would greatly increase the number of murders, hospital admissions, and accidents that month. He was right! In fact, in Dade County, Florida, the murder toll in January 1974 increased even more than he thought it would—a whopping 300 percent!

Is More Evidence Needed?

Psychiatrist Alex Pokorny at Baylor College of Medicine in Texas wanted to test Dr. Lieber's conclusions. He conducted his own test in Houston, Texas, but he did not find a significant rise in the rate of crime at the time of the new or full moon. He wrote in the *American Journal of Psychiatry*, "Until other and more convincing evidence is presented, we believe the effect of the moon phases on homicide, suicide, and mental illness should be viewed as a myth."

Psychologist Schlossberg says that the moon probably does affect how people behave—but only because people think that it will. "From the time we're kids," he says, "we see those horror movies with the full moon and the clouds piercing it. We look for effects of the moon and we find them. We talk ourselves into it."

Clearly, scientists do not all agree about whether the moon really causes behaviors to change. That is why some professionals have done tests on people and animals to see if predictable,

"There is actually a physical influence of the moon upon the earth and its creatures, its tides and our own interior tides."

Joseph Campbell, *The Masks of God: Primitive Mythology*

"Psychologically, the moon definitely affects people. From the time we're kids, we see those horror movies with the full moon and the clouds piercing it. We look for effects of the moon and we find them. We talk ourselves into it."

Harvey Schlossberg, psychologist

Lon Chaney Jr. plays the tormented werewolf in the 1940 Hollywood film *The Wolfman.* The attention Hollywood has given to lycanthropy and lunacy has ensured that werewolves and the mystery of the full moon continue to remain a part of modern folklore.

dramatic physical changes occur in the body when the moon is in certain phases.

The Ebb and Flow of Body Tides

Dr. Lieber has tested the psychological responses people and animals have to the moon. He says that the moon influences human behavior in large part because of tides. He is not talking about ocean tides, but the tides that exist in our own bodies.

"Life has, I believe, biological high tides and low tides governed by the moon," he says. "At new and full moon, these tides are at their highest—and the moon's effect on our behavior is the strongest."

The human body is about 80 percent water. Most of this water is found in our cells, in the tissue

"Life has, I believe, biological high tides and low tides governed by the moon. At new and full moon, these tides are at their highest—and the moon's effect on our behavior is the strongest."

Arnold Lieber, *The Lunar Effect: Biological Tides and Human Emotions*

"The moon causes tides only in unbounded bodies of water like the world's oceans. Bounded bodies of water, such as land-locked lakes, unless they are very large (like the Great Lakes), are negligibly influenced. Clearly the water contained in the human body falls into the 'bounded waters' category."

I.W. Kelly, James Rotton, and Roger Culver, *Skeptical Inquirer, Winter 1985-86*

outside our cells, and in our blood. Some scientists believe that the same gravitational forces that create ocean tides create tides inside us, in the water that makes up most of our body. They say all people have their own internal high and low tides, which are governed by the moon.

At sea, when the sun, earth, and moon are aligned, the highest tides occur. Similarly, at the time of the full moon, people's internal tides may be at their highest. During people's high tides, say some scientists, more water collects in their cells, tissues, and blood, and can cause them to feel bloated, heavy, or depressed. Electromagnetic and gravitational forces may upset people emotionally, making them moody and irritable. Violent crimes increase. People who suffer from mental illness become worse, and maybe, just maybe, werewolves appear.

High Tide

Scientists have found strong proof that some animal behavior is affected by tides. Sea creatures, for instance, are greatly affected by the moon because their environment is controlled by the tides. Sea anemones, clams, mussels, and other animals that do not move around much in the water must rely on high tides to carry in a fresh supply of food for them. Other sea animals, such as the silver grunion fish, depend on the moon for their reproduction cycle. They wait for the high tide to carry them ashore, where they have only a few hours before they must wriggle back to sea. If they are not fast enough and the tide becomes too low, the water will be too shallow for them to navigate.

Dr. Frank Brown, a biologist, performed a famous study to determine how the moon's gravitational pull affects certain animals. He took oysters from their home in the waters of New Haven, Connecticut, and moved them a thousand miles away to a location outside of Chicago. The oysters were housed in laboratory trays with just enough salt water to barely cover their shells. Monitors were set up to keep the light and temperature constant. For two weeks the oysters continued to open their shells to feed according to the tidal movement of their former home at the seashore—even though the water level in their trays remained constant. But by the end of two weeks, every oyster had changed its cycle and was opening its shell when the moon was at its highest point over their new location near Chicago. In other words, even though the oyster's environment remained constant, the moon's influence was so strong that the oysters changed their eating pattern to match their new location.

Despite studies like Brown's, many critics do not believe the moon can affect people. They say our bodily "oceans" are not big enough. "I'm never affected by the moon, and I'm only affected by the tide if I want to go out in a rowboat," said scientist and science fiction writer Isaac Asimov.

Sociologist and mythologist Joseph Campbell held a different view. "There is actually a physical influence of the moon upon the earth and its creatures, its tides and our own interior tides," he said.

Scientist and science fiction writer Isaac Asimov did not believe that the moon could affect human behavior.

Where is the Proof?

Does the moon make some people become mad? Scientists disagree on the answer because no one has found a way to prove absolutely whether it does or not. Until someone does, what people conclude will depend on what research and statistics they choose to believe. As astronomer Phillip Ianna said, "Given the existing evidence, the question of a possible lunar influence must remain open."

Epilogue

The Search Goes On

(Opposite page) The visor of *Apollo 11* astronaut Edwin Aldrin's space suit reflects the lunar landing module and his fellow astronauts as he poses for this historic photograph. Did this and successive historic landings dispel the moon's age-old mystery?

To go to the moon! People have dreamed of this ever since they first looked up and wondered if the white ball of light that illuminated the night sky could be reached, touched, or even walked upon. In the midtwentieth century, that dream came true.

In 1959 *Luna II*, a Soviet space capsule, became the first spacecraft to touch down on the moon. This was the first victory in the space race, sparked by the Soviet-American competition of the Cold War.

In 1961 American president John F. Kennedy said, "Now is the time to take longer strides. . . . I believe that this nation should commit itself to the goal, before this decade is out, of landing a man on the moon and returning him safely to earth."

In 1969 the United States did just that. American astronauts Edwin Aldrin and Neil Armstrong landed and walked on the moon's Sea of Tranquility. They collected rock samples that have taught us much about what the moon is made of. But many questions remain unanswered.

Benefits of Moon Exploration

Some people believe permanent lunar laboratories should be set up on the moon. The moon has no atmosphere and it would be easier to study other

stars and planets from its clear sky than from the earth's often hazy atmosphere. Learning about other constellations and solar systems may teach us about the earth's birth—and maybe even about our solar system's future thousands or millions of years from now.

Critics of the space program say we should spend the millions of dollars allocated to it to improve people's lives on earth. "If America fails to end discrimination, hunger, and malnutrition, then we must conclude that America is not committed to

The giant *Saturn 5* rocket of the *Apollo 11* mission lifts off on July 16, 1969, carrying the first humans to the moon. Will—should—humans one day colonize the mysterious and ancient ruler of the night?

ending discrimination, hunger, and malnutrition," says attorney Sylvia Drew. "Walking on the moon proves that we can do what we want as a nation."

Key to the Future

Proponents of the space program, such as science fiction writer Ben Bova, say that lunar exploration holds the key to the future and may eventually make life better for people on earth. Bova says,

> Most politicians still see space as a luxury, a scientific adventure, an avenue for international prestige. Something that's nice, if you can afford it, but certainly not as vital to the nation's interests as defense, or crime, or welfare.

> They do not see the connection between the advances we make in space technology and the strength of the U.S. economy. In an era where the old smokestack industries have nearly collapsed under the pressure of international competition, where Japan and other nations are outdoing us in everything from automobiles to copying machines, our politicians do not understand that space technologies offer the main hope for the economy over the coming decades.

In fact, Bova adds, "Our goal should be to extend human society throughout the inner solar system. We must . . . begin focusing on expanding the frontier that begins a hundred miles overhead."

Will such exploration solve the many mysteries of the moon? It is hard to say. Even with today's advanced scientific equipment and techniques, the moon, in some ways, remains as mysterious and magical as it was to our ancestors thousands of years ago.

Glossary

apogee   when the moon is farthest from the earth.

astronomy   the science that studies objects in space.

blue moon   when two full moons occur in the same month. It can also refer to a moon that looks blue. This may happen just before sunrise or after sunset when dust or smoke is in the air.

crescent moon   the phase just before and after the new moon.

dark moon   the new moon.

earthshine   a dull reddish glow on the surface of the moon that can be seen during lunar eclipses. It is caused by reflected light from the earth.

full moon   when the entire face of the moon is lit.

gibbous moon   this phase occurs just after the first quarter and just before the last quarter.

honeymoon   an ancient German custom. The entire community celebrated the month after a wedding by drinking honey mead.

intercalation   aligning a lunar calendar with the solar year by adding extra days or months.

lunar eclipse   when the earth moves between the sun and the moon. A lunar eclipse occurs only when the moon is full.

lunar month   about 29.5 days. Also called a lunation or synodic month.

mare   the Latin word for sea. It is a dark feature on the surface of the moon, formed by overflowing lava.

meteorite   an object in space that reaches the surface of a planet or the moon.

moon   the earth's natural satellite.

moonbow   similar to a rainbow, it is formed when moonlight passes through raindrops. It may be seen when the moon is full.

moondog   pale images of the moon off to one side of the moon. This phenomenon is caused by moonlight and moisture in the air.

moon pillars   shafts of light that appear above and below the moon.

moonraker   British country people saw the reflection of the moon in a pond and tried to rake it out, thinking it was a cheese. They were called "moonrakers."

moonrise   when the upper curve of the moon is visible in the east.

moonset   when the upper curve of the moon is visible in the west.

moonstone   a whitish, cloudy gemstone that is supposed to contain an image of the moon. Hindus thought it was formed when moonbeams congealed.

new moon   when the moon is between the earth and the sun. No light is reflected from its surface.

perigee   when the moon is closest to earth.

phases   the changes in the moon that occur every lunar month.

quarter moon   one quarter of the moon is visible.

revolution   the movement of a body around another body in an orbit.

rotation   the spinning of a body around its axis, an imaginary line that runs through its center.

solar eclipse   the moon comes between the earth and the sun, blocking out the sun.

tides   the movement of bodies of water caused by the gravitational pull of the earth, sun, and moon.

waning moon   the moon is moving from full to new. The size of the moon is decreasing.

waxing moon   the moon is moving from new to full. The size of the moon is increasing.

For Further Exploration

Keith Deutsh, *Space Travel: In Fact and Fiction*. New York: Franklin Watts, 1980.

Roy Gallant, *Exploring the Moon*. New York: Doubleday & Company, 1966.

Eric Hadley and Tessa Hadley, *Legends of the Sun and Moon*. New York: Cambridge University Press, 1983.

T.A. Heppenheimer, *Colonies in Space*. New York: Warner Books, 1978.

Henry King, *Moon Rocks*. New York: Dial Press, 1970.

Patricia Lauber, *Journey to the Planets*. New York: Crown Publishers, 1982.

Kim Long, *The Moon Book*. Boulder, CO: Johnson Books, 1988.

Jacqueline Mitten and Simon Mitten, *Discovering Astronomy*. Mahwah, NJ: Troll Associates, 1982.

Miriam Schlein, *Juju-Sheep and the Python's Moonstone*. Morton Grove, IL: Albert Whitman & Co., 1973.

Dorothy E. Shuttlesworth and Lee Ann Williams, *The Moon: Steppingstone to Outer Space*. New York: Doubleday & Company, 1977.

G. Jeffrey Taylor, *A Close Look at the Moon*. New York: Dodd, Mead & Company, 1980.

Jules Verne, *From the Earth to the Moon*. New York: Dodd, Mead & Company, 1959.

Wernher von Braun, *First Men to the Moon*. New York: Holt, Rinehart & Winston, 1960.

Tom Wolfe, *The Right Stuff*. New York: Farrar, Straus & Giroux, 1979.

Additional Sources

Books

Peter Adams, *Moon, Mars, and Meteorites.* London: British Geological Survey, 1977.

David Adler, *All About the Moon.* Mahwah, NJ: Troll Associates, 1983.

Necia H. Apfel, *The Moon and its Exploration.* New York: Franklin Watts, 1986.

Isaac Asimov, *The Earth's Moon.* Milwaukee: Gareth Stevens Publishing, 1988.

Anthony Aveni, *Empires of Time: Calendars, Clocks, and Cultures.* New York: Basic Books, 1989.

Anne Bancroft, *Origins of the Sacred: The Way of the Sacred in Western Tradition.* New York: Arkana, 1987.

Rhoda Blumberg, *The First Travel Guide to the Moon.* New York: Four Winds Press, 1980.

Franklyn M. Branley, *Pieces of Another World: The Story of the Moon Rocks.* New York: Thomas Y. Crowell Company, 1972.

Peter Lancaster Brown, *Megaliths, Myths, and Men.* New York: Taplinger Publishing Company, 1976.

Joseph Campbell, *The Masks of God: Primitive Mythology.* New York: Penguin Books, 1969.

Heather Cooper and Nigel Henbest, *The Moon.* New York: Franklin Watts, 1986.

Esther M. Harding, *Women's Mysteries: Ancient and Modern.* London: Rider & Company, 1972.

Fred Hoyle, *On Stonehenge.* San Francisco: W.H. Freeman and Company, 1977.

Paul Katzeff, *Full Moons.* New York: Citadel Press, 1983.

E.C. Krupp, *Echoes of the Ancient Skies: The Astronomy of Lost Civilizations.* New York: New American Library, 1983.

Arnold Lieber, *The Lunar Effect: Biological Tides and Human Emotions.* New York: Anchor Press/Doubleday & Co., 1978.

Walter A. McDougall, *. . . the Heavens and the Earth: A Political History of the Space Age.* New York: Basic Books, 1985.

Norman Mailer, *Of a Fire on the Moon.* Boston: Little, Brown & Company, 1969.

Patrick Moore, *Armchair Astronomy.* New York: W.W. Norton & Co., 1984.

Ross P. Olney, *They Said It Couldn't Be Done.* New York: E.P. Dutton, 1979.

Louise Riotte, *Planetary Planting.* New York: Simon & Schuster, 1975.

Anne Kent Rush, *Moon. Moon.* New York: Random House, 1976.

Wernher von Braun, Silvio A. Bedini, and Fred L. Whipple, *Moon: Man's Greatest Adventure.* New York: Harry N. Abrams, 1979.

Barbara G. Walker, *The Woman's Dictionary of Symbols and Sacred Objects.* San Francisco: Harper & Row, 1988.

Hamilton Wright, Helen Rapport, and Samuel Rapport, eds., *To the Moon.* New York: Meredith Press, 1968.

Articles

Naomi Bluestone, "Lunar Tricks," *Health*, October 1985.

Alan P. Boss, "The Origin of the Moon," *Science*, January 24, 1985.

Ben Bova, "Full (Moon) Employment," *Space World*, August 1988.

Ben Bova, "The Either/Or Fallacy," *Analog Science Fiction*, July 1989.

Bill Brogdon, "Secrets of the Telltale Moon," *Motor Boating and Sailing*, November 1982.

Robert Burham, "How Apollo Changed the Moon," *Astronomy*, July 1989.

Leonard David, "Moon Fever," *Space World*, August 1988.

Bod Diehl and Dorothy Diehl with Bryce Walden, "A Weekend in the Moon," *Space World*, December 1988.

William Farrand, "Will Moon Dust become the Gold Dust of the 21st Century?" *Ad Astra*, February 1989.

Arthur Fisher, "Birth of the Moon," *Popular Science*, Juauary 1987.

Arthur Fisher, "Moon Birth," *Popular Science*, October 1986.

"Fletcher Supports Moon Outpost by 2004," *Ad Astra*, January 1989.

Lance Frazer, "Lunar Lucre," *Space World*, August 1988.

Ralph Gardner Jr., "The Mania of the Full Moon," *Cosmopolitan*, June 1983.

Harold Gilliam, "Shine On, Harvest Moon," *This World*, October 4, 1987.

William K. Hartmann, "Birth of the Moon," *Natural History*, November 1989.

"How Do Moon Rocks Fall to Earth?" *Science Digest*, August 1983.

"Lunar Observatory," *Space World*, September 1984.

"The Making of a Better Moon," *Sky and Telescope*, December 1986.

Ron Miller and Frederick C. Durant III, "Lunar Fantasies," *Omni*, February 1987.

"The Moon Influences Western U.S. Drought," *Science*, May 11, 1984.

"Moon Madness No Myth," *Science Digest*, March 1981.

"Moon Teller," *Space World*, March 1985.

Cable Neuhaus, "There's More to Full Moon Mania than Horror Film Monsters, Warns Researcher Ralph Morris," *People*, May 10, 1982.

Robert G. Nichols, "From Footprints to Foothold," *Astronomy*, July 1989.

Alcestis Oberg, "Home on the Moon," *Scientific Digest*, October 1983.

"One Small Drop for Man," *Discover*, March 1988.

Devera Pine, "The Lunar Geosciences Orbiter Mission," *Space World*, November 1984.

Bridget Mintz Register, "The Fate of the Moon Rocks," *Astronomy*, December 1985.

Stephen Solomon, "Space," *Scientific Digest*, October 1983.

Dietrick E. Thomsen, "Man in the Moon," *Science News*, March 8, 1986.

"Was the Moon Formed by a Giant Collision?" *Astronomy*, July 1986.

"Winnebago Moonwatcher," *Discover*, May 1985.

Ed Zern, "Exit Laughing," *Field and Stream*, March 1981.

Index

About the Author

Patricia Haddock is a full-time writer and communications consultant living in San Francisco. She is insatiably curious and has written about a wide variety of topics, from animal superstitions to mythological monsters to business issues. This is her first book in the Great Mysteries series.

Picture Credits